THE INVISIBLE LINE

The Truth About Visibility, Authority, and the Bullshit No One Warns You About

WENDY BABCOCK

WHEN Stories Media Group

Contents

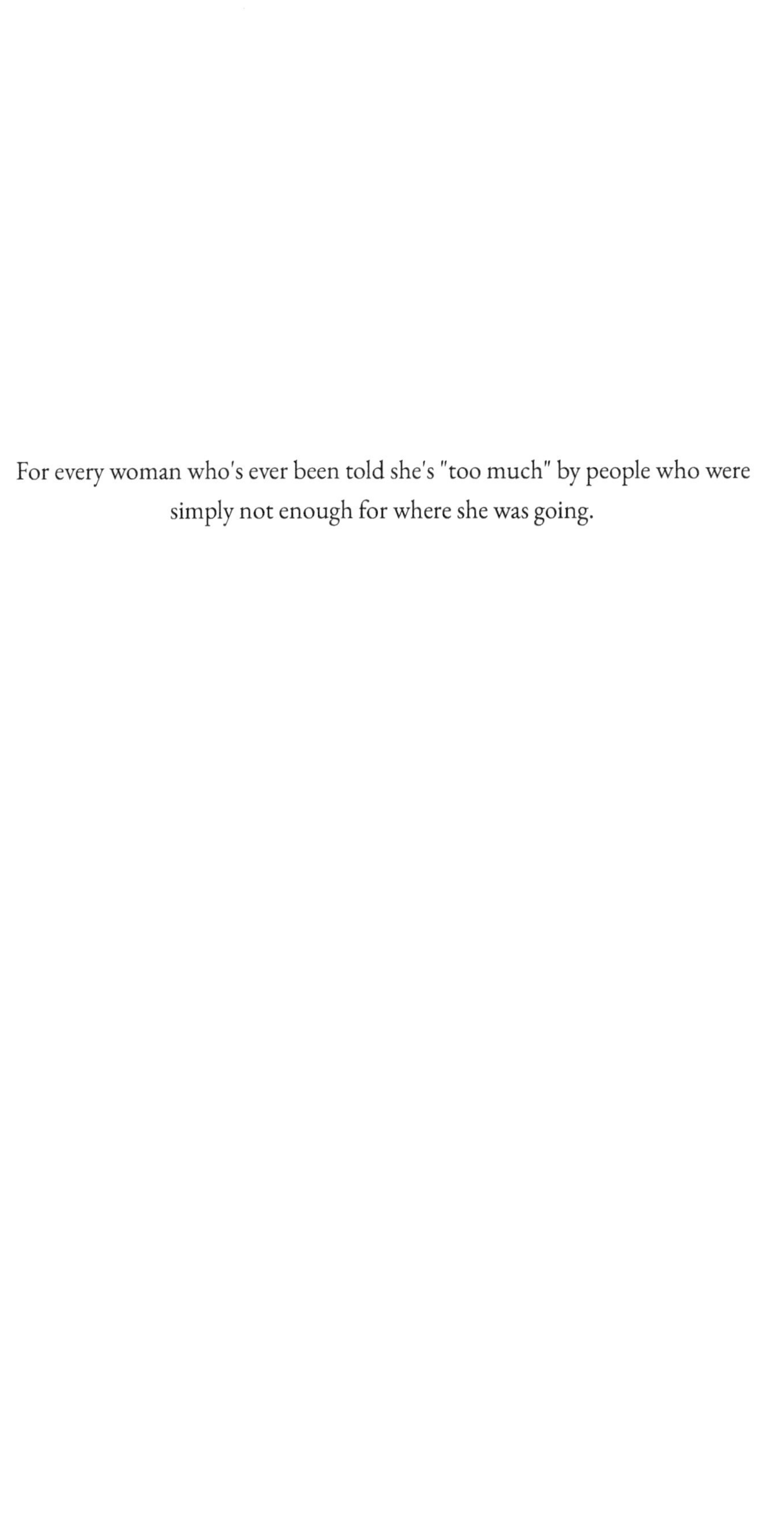

For every woman who's ever been told she's "too much" by people who were simply not enough for where she was going.

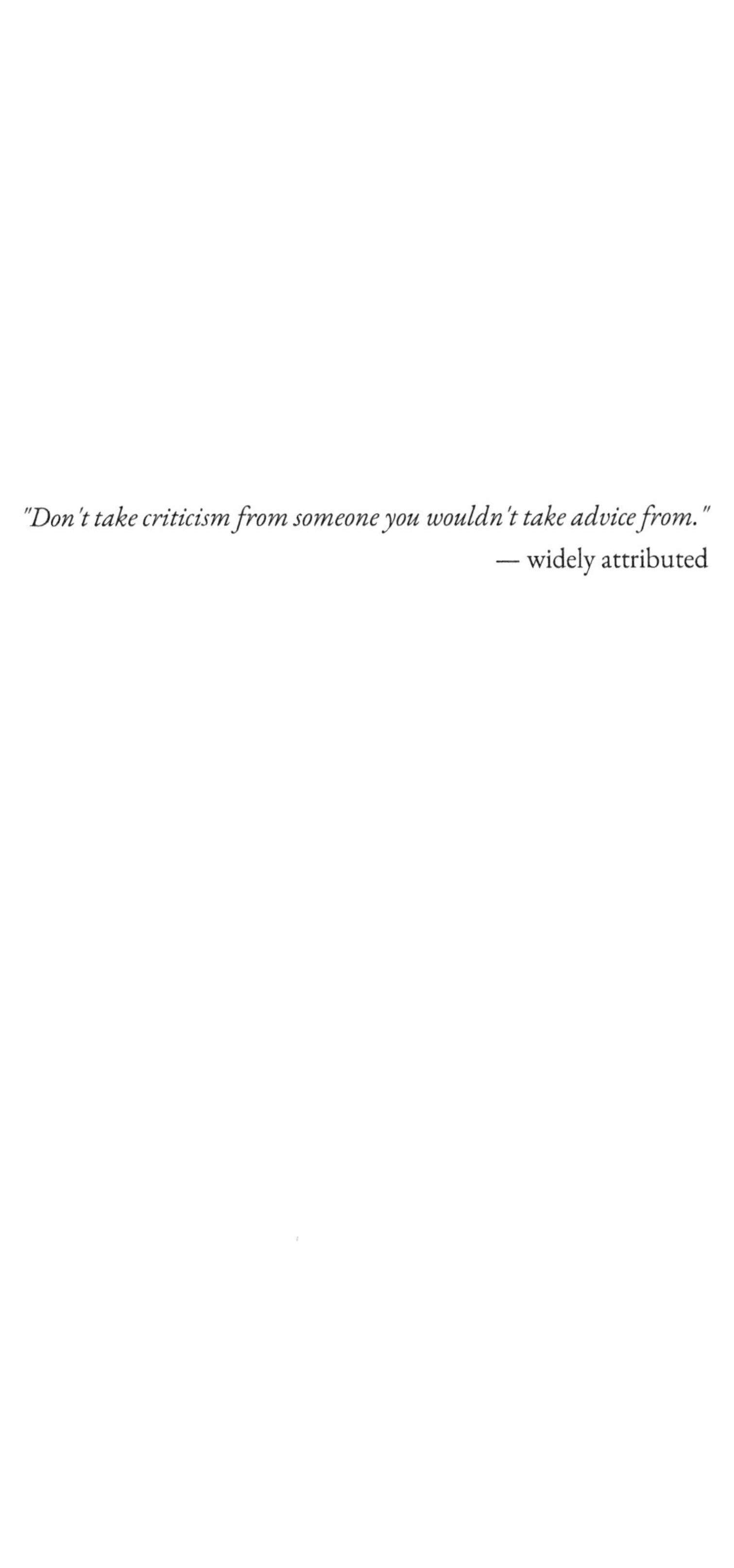

"Don't take criticism from someone you wouldn't take advice from."
— widely attributed

Introduction
THe invisible Line

There's a moment in every woman's business where everything shifts.

You can't see it coming. There's no announcement. No warning sign. No one pulls you aside and says, "Hey, things are about to get weird."

But you feel it.

The friend who used to cheer you on goes quiet. The networking group that felt like home starts to feel like a courtroom. Someone you trusted says something behind your back that makes your stomach drop. The very people who told you to "go for it" are now whispering about whether you've gotten too big for your britches.

You haven't changed. Your values are the same. Your intentions are still good. You're still the same woman who started this whole thing because she wanted to help people.

But the way people see you has shifted.

And you can't figure out what you did wrong.

I know this feeling because I've lived it — more than once.

It started in a third-grade classroom, where a teacher used his authority to humiliate me in front of my classmates. It showed up years later when I built a

Facebook group about kindness that grew to thousands of members in days — and almost overnight, the people I thought were friends turned on me. It followed me into networking rooms, onto speaking stages, through coaching calls, and into the business I eventually built from the ground up.

Every time I grew, the line appeared.

Every time I crossed it, someone made me pay.

And every time, I thought it was my fault.

This book is about that line — the invisible one that sits between "You go, girl!" and "Who the hell does she think she is?"

It's the line between being a peer and being perceived as an authority. Between being supported and being scrutinized. Between being one of the group and being the one the group talks about.

For women especially, this line is brutal. Because we're taught to be collaborative, humble, and generous. We're taught to share the credit, stay accessible, and never act like we think we're better than anyone else. And then we build something successful and discover that the rules we followed to get here are the exact rules that make us a target once we arrive.

That's the paradox at the heart of this book: you need authority to succeed, but claiming it activates forces that work against you. You aim for visibility and credibility — and when you get it, the ground shifts beneath your feet.

I didn't write this book because I have all the answers. I wrote it because I spent years not understanding the question.

Why do people change when you grow?

Why does success feel dangerous instead of celebratory?

Why do the women who were supposed to be your people become the ones who hurt you the most?

And — the question nobody wants to ask — why do we do it to each other?

This book answers those questions. Not with theories from a distance, but with stories from the middle of it. My stories. My mistakes. My blind spots. The moments I shrank when I should have stood. The moments I didn't realize I was drawing an invisible line around someone else's success while complaining about the one drawn around mine.

Here's what you'll find in the pages ahead.

The first half of this book is about understanding the invisible line — what it is, why it exists, and why it hits women in business so hard. You'll learn what authority actually means (and why that word makes most of us flinch). You'll see what happens when you claim it accidentally and how the people around you react in predictable, painful ways. You'll understand how proximity — the closeness that once felt like connection — can quietly erode the very authority you're trying to build. And you'll confront the uncomfortable truth that the invisible line isn't just something that happens *to* you. It's something you do to other women too.

The second half is about navigating it. How to build the kind of visibility that compounds instead of exhausts. How to be intentional about who sees your growth and who sees your process. How to claim your authority without apologizing for it. How to handle the moment when the temperature changes and the people you trusted start pulling away. And how to build a business that doesn't require you to shrink yourself to make everyone else comfortable.

This isn't a book about avoiding authority. It's not a book about becoming untouchable or building walls around your success.

It's a book about understanding what happens when you grow — so you can keep growing without losing yourself or the people who matter in the process.

My journey started in a third-grade classroom with an accordion folder and a tape recorder. It continued through speaking stages, viral Facebook posts, music awards, and a business I built from a daydream at my desk. Along the way, I learned that authority isn't granted — it's felt. Proximity isn't always connection — sometimes it's erosion. Visibility isn't one thing — it's two. And the invisible line doesn't care how good your intentions are.

It shows up anyway.

So let's start at the beginning.

PART ONE

THE MAKING OF AUTHORITY ANXIETY

CHAPTER 1

April Fools

Authority is the power or right to give orders, make decisions, and be believed.

I've always struggled with authority.

My stomach tightens. I put my head down. I shrink.

This pattern started early, and like most patterns that shape us, I didn't recognize it until much later.

Mr. Kennedy, my third-grade teacher, ran his classroom like a business.

At the beginning of the year, he passed out ugly brown accordion file folders with three sections and a rubber band that looped around to hold them closed. We were to use these to keep our papers separated: Reading, Writing, Arithmetic.

The folder was to be kept on the right side of our desks on the floor, standing upright. No papers were ever to be placed inside our desks. He was strict about this. Inside your desk must be kept tidy at all times.

He made me nervous. His voice, when raised, was a loud, booming, deep bellow. I rarely recall him raising it, because I'm sure all the other third graders, like me, were too intimidated.

On Mondays, he had everyone walk over to the side of the room and speak into an almost rectangular but rounded silver microphone with a flat top, attached by a cord to an old tape player on a standalone round table. Each week, one by one, each child nervously spoke into the microphone and talked about what they did over the weekend.

He recorded every one of these.

When my name was called, there was an instant lump in my throat. I walked over, picked up the microphone, and began to tell my weekend stories.

To this day, I have no recollection of any of them.

Home life back then wasn't exactly pleasant. It wouldn't have occurred to me to announce that maybe I'd been beaten with a belt for waking up my stepfather from his nap, or that my sister ended up with a bloody nose from being smacked in the back of the head.

So I imagine my stories were more mundane—playing Barbies with my sister or being outside all weekend with neighborhood kids.

The desks were arranged in a square, with all the students facing each other. The front of the room had a blackboard—that was really green—with lots of chalk dust, and it always had the day and date neatly written on it. There was a cartoon character next to the blackboard with a quote beside it. I wish I could remember what it was, because it felt like a classroom mascot.

In the back of the room, another blackboard had the entire class's names written in two columns, alphabetically by last name. The room was tidy, organized, and aesthetically pleasing.

There was also a large paper chart on the back wall with all our last names in a single column and three columns to the right: Reading, Writing, and Arithmetic. When you finished your work each week, you received a star sticker in that column. The colors were gold, red, or blue.

I have no idea what his system was. All I know is that it created anxiety—that my columns wouldn't get a star and I would feel embarrassed.

Just before spring break that year, Mr. Kennedy handed out very large packets of papers, all stapled together at the top left corner. The instructions were to take them home over spring break and complete all of it.

I remember thumbing through the packet, feeling uneasy. I didn't have confidence that I could get it all done. It was spring break—who wanted to spend the whole week doing homework?

Like a typical third grader, I forgot about it entirely.

Saturday morning came, and I flushed with panic.

The packet. I forgot.

I knew I'd have to work really hard to complete it. I sat at the kitchen table, almost in tears, frantically working through the writing portions and math problems.

By Sunday night, I still wasn't done, and my parents noticed the tears running down my face.

My mom sat on my left. My stepdad sat on my right. They both swore and complained—about my not starting sooner, about the size of the packet, about the absurdity of sending it home over a break.

It was at least an hour past my bedtime when I finished the last page. I was exhausted. I crawled into bed, pulled the covers over me, and fell asleep.

The next morning, I walked into the classroom with my brown accordion file folder under my arm. I walked to the far row of desks, sat down, pulled out the large packet, set it on my desk, placed my accordion file on the floor to the right...

...and waited.

Mr. Kennedy was unusually chipper that morning.

"Okay, let's see those packets on your desks. Who didn't get theirs completed?"

Everyone looked around nervously. Yet every packet sat neatly on every desk, ready to be picked up.

"Everyone finished?" he asked, sounding surprised.

Then a loud, almost maniacal laugh burst from him.

"April Fools!"

We were all confused.

"April Fools! I can't believe you all finished that packet!"

He laughed hysterically. He was the only one laughing.

Suddenly, I felt a tightness behind my eyes. My nose started to tingle—the familiar sign I was about to cry.

When I got home, my parents asked if I turned my packet in.

"Yes... but it was an April Fools joke."

I hung my head, fighting tears.

"What the fuck?!" my stepdad shouted.

"What kind of bullshit is that?!" my mom joined in.

The next thing I remember is my mom calling the school the next day to give Mr. Kennedy a piece of her mind. One of the very few times she stood up for me.

I was afraid to go to school after that. But surprisingly, Mr. Kennedy seemed to shrug it off. I'm guessing he received more than a few phone calls like the one from my mom.

The weirdest thing we had to do in that class was his year-long assignment.

At the beginning of the year, we were told to choose one of two options: memorize all the students' last names in alphabetical order and recite them into the tape recorder, or memorize and recite the short story *This Is the House That Jack Built.*

Not knowing this would feed the overachiever I am today, I memorized both—just to be safe.

During the last week of school, when it was time to record our final entry into the silver microphone, I chose to recite the last names of all the students in alphabetical order.

Most of my classmates chose the short story. Some did it perfectly. Many forgot parts. One after another, they walked up, nervously spoke into the microphone, stumbled over their words, turned red, and sheepishly walked back to their desks.

Then it was my turn.

I had practiced so many times, I could have recited that list in my sleep.

Big deep breath.

"Aybaar, Costello, Gross, Hansen..."

I kept going.

"Lee, Maggio, Muhammed..."

The names came out one after another, like muscle memory.

"...Wethington and Woytovich."

Every. Single. Name.

I didn't miss a beat. I nailed all of them.

I walked back to my desk feeling like an absolute rockstar.

Fun fact: that was 1983. It's now 2026, and I can still recite every single last name—though don't quote me on the spellings.

But by the end of that year, I didn't feel confident. I felt unsure. I second-guessed myself constantly. Because even though I nailed the task, I stressed about it the entire year, thinking up all kinds of crazy scenarios of what might happen if I messed it up.

I learned that authority could humiliate you and call it a joke. That adults could hold power over you and not notice the impact at all.

That year, I was also hit in the head with a football. I was knocked out. I woke up in the nurse's office, alone. I had no idea how I got there. My head hurt and I felt sick to my stomach.

I got up and walked back to my classroom. A couple of kids quietly asked if I was okay, but I didn't know why they were asking. No one had told me what happened.

Later that day, we had an assembly. About five minutes in, I knew I was going to throw up. I stood up and sprinted back to the nurse's office, where I threw up into a large garbage can.

They called my mom to come get me because I was "sick."

No one seemed to have information about me being knocked out cold during recess.

My head was throbbing. I rubbed the side where it hurt and noticed a large lump. Then another one on the other side.

I told my mom. She took me to the hospital.

Double concussion.

It was a hell of a year.

I bring up the head injury because I realized the people who were supposed to make sure I was safe didn't. When I woke up in the nurse's office and had no idea why I was there, there wasn't an adult—an authority—in sight.

Between the joke and the injury, something shifted. I didn't trust authority the same way anymore—but I didn't trust myself either. My body didn't feel reliable. My instincts felt questionable. Even my thoughts felt like something I needed to double-check.

I learned to stay alert. To be careful. To watch for the moment when something that was supposed to be safe suddenly wasn't.

I didn't have words for any of that back then.

I just knew the ground felt less solid than it had before.

What I didn't realize then—what I wouldn't understand for decades—was that this early experience with authority set a pattern.

Authority became something to fear. Something unpredictable. Something that could turn on you without warning. Or something that could let you down and not be available when you needed it.

And when you grow up fearing authority, you develop an interesting relationship with it as an adult.

You want it—because it promises safety, control, credibility.

But you're terrified of it—because you remember what happens when someone has power over you.

That contradiction would follow me for years. Through my career, my speaking journey, my businesses. I would chase authority and then sabotage it the moment I got close.

Because deep down, I believed that becoming the authority meant becoming Mr. Kennedy. And I never wanted to be him.

CHAPTER 2

All Eyes on Me

The moment you become visible, you become vulnerable.

Between third grade and becoming a professional speaker, I didn't lose my fear of authority.

I just went from being too young to name it to being a grown-ass adult who finally realized: oh, this is still a thing.

In 2017, I was working as an outpatient medical coder. I didn't love my job, but it paid the bills. I had only become a coder out of necessity—when transcription was outsourced, I was offered a new position so I could stay employed.

Medical coding is numbers and diagnoses. I memorized the codes to make the job go quicker. And as you could probably guess from my third-grade Olympic-level memorization skills, this made my job much easier.

Almost too easy. And far too mundane.

The repetitiveness made me want to smash my head into the wall. Being surrounded by three walls at all times, stuck in a tiny cubicle—yeah, it was tempting.

What I haven't told you yet is that I'm very much an undiagnosed ADHD, neurodivergent type of gal. If I don't have squirrels to chase, shiny new ideas to obsess over, and at least three of my ten trains of thought going off the rails at any given moment, I tend to wander off into Never Never Land.

What really worked for me was listening to audiobooks while I worked.

I know—it sounds crazy to do detailed work and listen to audiobooks at the same time. But I listened to personal development books, so it wasn't like I had to follow a plot. It was just enough information to keep one part of my brain busy so I could focus on work instead of thinking about dinner, my restless left foot, whether my oldest daughter remembered her homework, or if my younger daughter had volleyball practice or rehearsal after school.

There was always noise in my brain. Audiobooks fixed that.

One freezing cold Wisconsin day in January 2017, I happened to tune into a particular part of Pam Grout's book *E-Squared* where she talked about wondering what could go right instead of obsessing over what was going wrong.

She mentioned a movement called A Complaint Free World, where the founder, Will Bowen, helps people get out of the never-ending complaining loop.

I was intrigued.

At that point in my life, I'd done therapy to deal with PTSD from childhood trauma and an abusive first marriage. I was finally happy, married to my favorite person on the planet, and genuinely trying to find the good in everyday life. So the moment I heard A Complaint Free World, it resonated deeply.

I went straight to Google. After scouring the website, I headed over to social media and followed Will Bowen.

What happened next was one of those "when" moments—you know, the moment when everything changes.

I pulled up Will's Facebook page, and the very first post at the top of his feed was a call for people interested in sharing the Complaint Free World message. He would train you, and you'd get on stages—like he does—and share it with the world.

I sat with that for a second.

Me? On stage? Speaking?

Yeah... I almost threw up from the anxiety—and excitement—just thinking about it.

What the heck, right? Why not? I probably wouldn't even be chosen anyway. I had no doubt thousands of people would apply, judging by the sheer number of comments on the post.

I pushed send.

The email—explaining a little about myself, how I came across the post, and why I felt called to share the message—was off through the internet to Will Bowen's assistant's inbox.

Suddenly, I had a flashback to standing in front of my third-grade class, silver microphone in hand, completely blanking as I spoke into that tape recorder.

What the hell was I thinking?

I laughed it off, shrugged, and assumed the email would disappear into the abyss of someone's never-ending inbox.

Ding! You have mail.

An email from Will's assistant.

I scanned it quickly, fully expecting a form response along the lines of: "Thank you for applying. We received many applications and unfortunately, you were not chosen. Try again next time, loser."

Instead, it said something more like: "Hey there. We like you. Let's talk on Skype."

Well... not in those exact words.

After my call with Will's assistant—who also happened to be his daughter, Lia—I felt genuinely excited about the possibility of being chosen. Lia really listened to my story, asked thoughtful follow-up questions, and explained more about the training and what the program involved.

And yes—I was chosen for Will's program. No big plot twist here.

Myself and nine other "space monkeys," as Will and Lia lovingly called us, hit the ground running with his training. At the end of the 16-week program, Will invited us all to his home to become Certified Complaint Free World Trainers. We would go into a studio, give our presentations, and be recorded.

What I didn't realize until we walked into the studio was that Will Bowen himself was quite the tech guy—and he would be the one behind the camera.

Suddenly, I felt small again.

I felt like I was under a microscope, giving my presentation with my mentor—the actual founder of the movement—standing behind the camera, aimed directly at me.

Every word. Every movement. Every "um."

Carefully watched. Carefully judged.

That authority anxiety set in again.

This time, though, I embraced it.

Yes, I was nervous and wanted to vomit at least three separate times—but I kept telling myself I could do this.

Just remember your training. You're here. Don't waste this moment.

I gave my presentation. It wasn't perfect, but Will offered gentle guidance and feedback, and everyone gave me a big round of applause.

Here's what I wish someone had told me then:

Training doesn't prepare you for what happens after the applause.

Will's training was exceptional—genuinely the best I've ever seen. He didn't just give me a platform to teach; he taught me every step I needed to build a signature talk, apply for speaking opportunities, get paid, and everything in between.

He didn't miss a single thing.

And I can tell you this after nearly ten years of experience—I still haven't seen another program that thorough. It covered everything. On top of that, you weren't just trained... you became an extension of him.

And he's been on Oprah, for God's sake.

But here's what the training couldn't teach me: what happens when you step into that visibility.

Speaking opportunities came—and then they didn't. Some gigs paid well. Others were almost insulting in how they treated their speakers.

I learned a lot about myself during this time.

Not only did I feel the weight of authority push back on me, but for the first time, I also got to feel like the authority myself.

Standing on stage. All eyes on me. Leaning in. Listening.

And when I walked off that stage, I felt like that same rockstar—walking back to my desk after reciting every student's last name without missing a beat.

That feeling is intoxicating.

It's also dangerous.

Because what nobody tells you is that the moment you step into that spotlight, you activate something in the people watching.

Some of them will be inspired. Some will be supportive. Some will cheer you on.

And some—sometimes the same people who were just cheering—will start to feel something else entirely.

It's subtle at first. A shift in tone. A comment with an edge. A little less warmth than there used to be.

You tell yourself you're imagining it.

But you're not.

This is the first sign you've crossed the invisible line.

You've moved from being someone people relate to, to someone people react to.

From peer to authority.

And once that shift happens, visibility stops being an asset and starts becoming a liability.

The visibility game tells you to keep showing up. Keep posting. Keep being seen. Keep building your platform.

What it doesn't tell you is that every time you show up, you're reinforcing a hierarchy that makes people uncomfortable.

You on stage. Them in the audience.

You with the microphone. Them listening.

You with the expertise. Them needing what you have.

Even when your message is about positivity, empowerment, or lifting others up—the act of delivering it from a position of authority creates distance.

And distance breeds resentment.

I didn't know this yet. I was still caught up in the high of being chosen, being trained, being on stages.

I didn't lose my fear of authority—I just got older, more capable, and better at pretending it wasn't there.

But it was about to come roaring back.

Because the next phase of my journey would teach me something critical about the invisible line:

It's not just about how authority makes you feel.

It's about how your authority makes everyone else feel.

And that's where things get complicated.

Let me unpack what was actually going on in this chapter—because it's easy to read this as a success story and miss the invisible line being drawn.

I got trained by someone who'd been on Oprah. That's proximity to authority.

I got certified. That's legitimacy.

I got on stages. That's visibility.

Every single one of these things is supposed to help you build your business and your influence. And they do—until they don't.

Here's the paradox: the same visibility that creates opportunities also creates targets. When you're on stage, you're not just sharing information. You're claiming space. You're positioning yourself as someone worth listening to. You're asserting authority. And the moment you do that, you invite judgment. Not just of your message, but of you. Of whether you deserve to be up there. Of whether you've earned the right to speak.

The more visible you become, the more scrutiny you face. The more success you have, the more people question whether you deserve it. The more authority you claim, the more resistance you encounter.

For women, this dynamic is particularly vicious. Research on what's called the "double bind" shows that women face competing expectations: be confident but not arrogant, be competent but not threatening, be visible but not too visible. The line between "inspiring" and "intimidating" is razor-thin, and you don't get to decide which side you're on. Other people decide for you.

This is why the visibility game is bullshit.

Not because visibility doesn't matter—it does. You can't build a speaking career or a thought leadership platform without it.

But because the advice to "just be more visible" ignores the social and psychological dynamics that activate the moment you step into the spotlight.

It assumes that more visibility equals more success.

What it actually equals is more exposure—and exposure cuts both ways.

CHAPTER 3

The Big Bad Word

The words we use to describe ourselves reveal which claims we're willing to make.

"I wrote a book, but I'm not an *author*," I insisted for months.

In January 2019, I made the decision to write a book. I put no expectations on it. It was simply about the process—learning how to do it and putting something out into the world that was mine.

Knowing myself, I knew if I didn't set a tough deadline, that book would never leave my brain and see the light of day. I pulled up my calendar and swiped through month to month. I stopped on April 2019.

Could I really write a book between January and April? I remember tilting my head, raising my eyebrows, looking up at the corner of the room. Could it be done?

Then I chuckled to myself as I picked the date: April 1, 2019. April Fools' Day it would be. (Ironic, now that I write this book and the first chapter was about April Fools' Day.)

I had a framework for the idea of the book. Was it great? No. But it was mine.

I loved everything about the Complaint Free World movement that I'd been speaking on stages about, but somewhere deep down, I really wanted my own thing.

Every day I would sit down and start typing away. Honestly, I didn't even have an outline. I had no idea where I was going with the book. I just knew if I started, I would make it work. I've really never been one to follow the rules anyway.

After I wrote the first chapter, I decided this was when I had to name the book.

I remember getting out a piece of paper and scribbling down everything and anything that came to mind. The book was two ideas pasted and duct-taped together. It was about dealing with assholes and trying to live a positive life despite them. See, with A Complaint Free World, Will's program taught you how to communicate better with people. Sometimes I'd get audience members who'd ask me, "But what if you're dealing with an asshole?" And while it was a funny question, it got me thinking...

What *do* you do when you have an encounter with an asshole and not have it ruin your entire day?

That was the spark for the book.

After about half an hour of scribbling, the book was officially titled: *How to Sparkle Where The Sun Don't Shine: Staying Positive When You're Surrounded by Assholes.*

In hindsight, sure it was clever, but it was long.

My ideas took shape. I researched the definition of "asshole" and how I wanted to define it so the reader knew I wasn't talking about someone abusive. The assholes I was talking about were the ones you'd never have an actual conversation with—the ones where the strategies I taught with the Complaint Free message wouldn't apply. These were the jerks who cut you off during your morning commute, the twerp at Starbucks who screwed up your order and you were in too much of a hurry to have them correct it, or the people at the grocery store with absolutely no spatial awareness who stand talking to an old neighbor and won't get the fuck out of the way so you can grab a loaf of bread and go home.

I asked people on social media about assholes they encountered to build up my ideas.

The next part was how to deal with them. This is where my framework came in. It was an acronym: FOCUS. Each letter stood for things you could do to stay positive when things weren't going your way.

I didn't have a "Sara" in my life back then. Sara Deacon is my business bestie (and my bestie bestie). She's the Head of Publishing for my business, WHEN Stories. She's a brilliant editor with a gift for details.

So when it came time to edit this masterpiece of a first book, I wasn't sure who was the right person. And at the time, resources were slim, so I had to do some bargain-basement editor hunting.

Someone mentioned a website where you could hire people for one-off jobs like this for pretty cheap, so that's what I did. I scoured the listings of editors, read some bios and descriptions, and basically played a game of Russian Roulette—closed my eyes and picked someone.

All in all, the woman I chose did an okay job, but I would never—and I mean *never*—hand that book to Sara to read. (Sara, if you're reading this, do NOT go read that book. I mean it.)

I did my due diligence about launching a book back then. They said to create a Facebook launch group, so I did. They said to create hype on social media, so I did. They said to take the readers along and give them some sneak peeks, so I did. Cover reveal? Yep, did that too.

April 1, 2019. Release day.

I had done it. I wrote a book. I put it out into the world. People actually bought it and read it. And they liked it.

Yes, there were typos. There were run-on sentences. It wasn't perfect. But it was out there.

"Congratulations! You're an author!" someone commented on Facebook.

"Oh, I'm not an author. Not like that. LOL! I just wrote a book. It's not a big deal."

Then a message hit my inbox.

"Wendy. You ARE an author."

I was?

No. *Real* authors write better than I do. I didn't go to college for this. I just... wrote a book.

I can't even express fully how that word haunted me.

AUTHOR.

I kept slapping it away anytime it came at me.

AUTHOR.

That's for *other* people who write books. Not me.

AUTHOR.

My book isn't even that good. It has typos.

AUTHOR.

I mean, I guess *technically*... I am. Right?

AUTHOR.

Okay, okay. I'm an author.

Seriously—how freaking silly is that? Why did I struggle with that word so much?

What I find fascinating now is that the words "author" and "authority" share the same Latin root: *auctor*. The person who creates. The originator.

I was literally an author, but I couldn't get past the word. I had assigned a meaning to it—something much deeper than what it actually was.

I started using it in my title and bio: *Wendy Babcock, Speaker and Author.* It felt so much more important. So impressive. *Wow, I kind of want to know who she is and what she's about.*

Only to be left feeling like... but I'm not that important. It made me feel like an imposter.

But why?

After all, I *was* an author.

If you noticed, my first response when someone called me an author was to say, "I'm a writer, not an author." It's the same flinch—reaching for the softer word. The one that doesn't require a claim.

To me, "writer" was a softer word. It didn't carry the weight of "author." But what was the actual difference?

"I'm a writer" says: I do this thing. It's a skill. A practice. It keeps you in the work, in the trenches, in the safe space of effort.

"I'm an author" says: I created something. I put my name on it. It exists in the world because of me. It's a declaration of ownership over your own intellectual contribution.

It's essentially *authority.*

Writer is the activity. Author is the identity. And identity is where we get squirmy—because identity is a *claim.* And claims feel dangerous.

The identity piece seems to trip up a lot of us.

Words like expert, influencer, thought leader, credibility, professional, consultant, coach, mentor, specialist—and the big bad word... authority.

Let's just break these words down in plain language definitions.

Expert—You know your stuff and people trust that you know your stuff.

Influencer—People change what they think or do because of you.

Thought leader—You're the person other people reference when they talk about your topic.

Credibility—People believe you when you speak. They trust your word.

Professional—You stood up and declared "this is what I do"—and people take you seriously for it.

Consultant—People pay you to tell them what you know.

Coach—People pay you to help them get better at something you're already good at.

Mentor—Someone trusts you enough to let you guide their decisions.

Specialist—You went deep instead of wide, and people seek you out because of it.

Authority—You've earned the right to be believed in your area through experience, contribution, or both.

Now look at that list again. Every single one of those words describes the same thing from a slightly different angle. Knowing your stuff. Being trusted. Being sought out. Guiding others. Creating something of value.

They're all *authority*.

Here's what's wild. When you look up the word "authority" in the dictionary, it doesn't just have one definition. It has several. And the difference between them is everything.

The first definition most people land on is "power to influence or command thought, opinion, or behavior."

Command. Power. Behavior.

Yeah. That's the one that makes your stomach tighten. That's the Mr. Kennedy definition. That's authority standing over you, telling you what to do, holding power you didn't ask to be under.

No wonder we flinch.

But keep reading.

Because the dictionary also defines authority as "a person with a high level of knowledge or skill in a field."

That's it. That's the whole definition. A person who knows their stuff.

Not a person who controls people. Not a person who dominates a room. Not a person who demands obedience.

A person who knows their stuff.

And "with authority" means "the confident quality of someone who knows a lot about something or who is respected by other people."

Go back even further to the 1828 Webster's Dictionary and you'll find authority defined as "the power derived from opinion, respect or esteem" and "weight of character; respectability; dignity."

Respect. Esteem. Dignity. Weight of character.

Does that sound like the scary word you've been avoiding?

The word has two faces. One is about power over people. The other is about earned knowledge, respect, and contribution.

And most of us have been running from the word based on the first definition while *living* the second definition every single day.

You have the knowledge. You have the respect. You have the credibility. You have the influence.

You just won't call it what it is—because the word feels like it belongs to the version of authority you're afraid of becoming.

Why do we do this? I'm speaking specifically to women entrepreneurs.

Why won't we claim the word authority? Stand up for what we have built? Why don't we embrace being the expert?

I wish I had a neat answer for you. But the truth is, I didn't figure this out by reading a definition or having some big lightbulb moment.

I figured it out the hard way—by accidentally stepping into authority and watching everything around me shift.

It started with a Facebook group about kindness. And it nearly broke me.

CHAPTER 4

Kill 'em With Kindness

Success doesn't just change how people see you. It changes what they project onto you.

"There's a post about you online... and it's not good."

My stomach dropped.

"What do you mean? Where? Why?"

"Yeah... people are coming for you over that group you started."

In August 2019, I started a Facebook group called The Kindness Bucket Brigade.

It all stemmed from a post I saw where a woman was being bullied in one of the local buy/sell/trade groups.

I noticed a comment from a friend. She didn't address any of the hate this poor woman was getting. She simply left a kind comment.

And it made me think: maybe if more people ignored the haters and added something kind, we could drown out the awful comments.

So I came up with the idea to start a group where members agreed that if one of us saw someone being bullied, we would leave a kind comment and tag another member of the group using the hashtag #kindnessbucketbrigade. That person would then comment and tag another member, creating a bucket brigade of kindness.

When I started the group, my goal was to eventually reach 100 members. I thought it would be absolutely amazing if that many people joined me.

To my surprise, we had over 200 members on the very first day.

By day four, we hit 1,000 members—and it was growing by the hour.

This is where I crossed the invisible line.

When something takes off faster than you expected, when growth happens exponentially instead of incrementally, when you go from invisible to highly visible overnight—that's when the invisible line appears.

You don't see it coming because you're focused on the good happening. On the messages pouring in. On the people saying "this is exactly what the world needs right now."

You don't realize you've crossed into authority territory until it's too late.

People from all over the world were joining, using the hashtag, and tagging other members. Eventually, I had to bring in moderators to help. We laid down some simple ground rules: no promotions, no bullying (obviously).

The content people shared was uplifting—stories of good deeds and paying it forward. The group overflowed with happy stories.

I was invited to news stations to do TV interviews. I was featured in local and statewide newspapers. The Kindness Bucket Brigade even made it into Reader's Digest.

With each TV broadcast or newspaper article, more people flooded into the group.

Soon, people began asking for prayer requests. Some were deeply personal. To help members feel safe, we made the decision to change the group from public to private.

The moderators and I had long conversations about every decision. We agreed that anyone who requested to join would be approved.

Then the complaints started.

"I shouldn't have to ASK to be in a kindness group! That's ridiculous!"

We put out statements explaining that this was simply how Facebook groups worked—and that everyone was welcome and approved right away.

"Oh, so this is like some gated community for kindness or something? No thanks."

"It's like they're running a cult in that kindness group."

Yeah. A lot of those comments got back to me. Screenshots were sent to me almost daily—snide remarks people were posting about the group.

Then came the big one. A whole thread. Pitchforks out.

"I think she's trying to brand kindness as her own or something. Like she thinks she owns kindness."

Comment after comment. I was shocked.

These weren't strangers.

These were people I knew. People in my community. People I was friends with.

I was sick to my stomach. I had no idea what I had done wrong. I simply wanted to help solve a problem. I never imagined the group would garner so much attention—both positive and negative.

I started living in a constant state of anxiety. My nervous system was on edge all the time.

Why were people so mad about this?

I couldn't make sense of it.

Around that same time, I started receiving speaking inquiries—mostly from schools. I thought, *Okay... here's something really positive. I could use my speaking skills to make a difference.*

After speaking at a few schools and a couple of local Boys & Girls Clubs, I started to get excited about the potential of a new direction for my speaking career.

Opportunities were coming to me through The Kindness Bucket Brigade. I didn't have to chase them down. It was such a rush.

Then one day...

"As your friend, I have to tell you—I really don't think this is your thing."

"What do you mean?"

"I know you really want to lean into this kindness thing, but I'm just not seeing it. I don't want to hurt your feelings or anything... I just don't think this is your thing."

This came from a close friend.

I was crushed.

Once again, I questioned everything.

Was everyone in on some secret but me? Was I living in an alternate universe?

I genuinely thought I was doing something good.

Day after day, I spent less time interacting with the group. I slowly stopped posting. Eventually, I stopped using the hashtag altogether.

You win. They all win. I give up.

What I didn't know then—but understand much better now—was that I had unknowingly stepped over an invisible line.

It was subtle... yet loud.

And everything changed.

That invisible line sat between "You go, girl!" and "Who the hell does she think she is?"

It was the line between being seen and becoming an authority.

When that realization hit, it felt like a punch to the gut.

To some people, I suddenly became the weird third-grade teacher or the mentor behind the camera. My ideas, my presence, the way I moved online—everything felt like it was under a microscope.

I'd experienced this before, when I was promoted to Lead Transcriptionist at the hospital. When you're in charge—even when you've had great relationships with coworkers—authority changes the game.

Now, you're the common enemy.

You're standing on the other side of that invisible line.

You're the authority.

But here's what made it even more confusing:

Not everyone turned on me.

Some people became more supportive. More engaged. More eager to be close to what was happening.

The group kept growing. The opportunities kept coming. The positive feedback was real.

So why did the negative voices feel so much louder?

Because they were unexpected.

When strangers criticize you, it stings. When friends do it, it breaks something.

And when you can't understand why it's happening—when you genuinely believe you're doing something good, and people are treating you like you've committed some unforgivable sin—you start to doubt your own reality.

That's the other side of the invisible line.

It makes you question yourself when you should be questioning the dynamics at play.

And once you cross that line, you have two choices: shrink back, make yourself smaller, and give up the authority you've claimed—or learn to operate with authority in a way that doesn't destroy you.

I chose the first one—because I didn't know the second one existed.

But giving up didn't solve the problem.

Because even after I stopped posting, even after I withdrew from the group, even after I tried to go back to being "just one of the girls"—the damage was done.

I had been seen. I had claimed authority, even briefly.

And you can't un-ring that bell.

The people who resented me didn't suddenly like me again.

The only thing that changed was how I felt about myself.

I went from excited and energized to anxious and defeated.

From confident in my vision to questioning everything.

From feeling like I was making a difference to feeling like I had made a terrible mistake.

That's what the invisible line does.

It makes you pay for your success with your peace of mind.

What I needed then—and what I want you to have now—is an understanding of the invisible dynamics at play when you step into authority.

Not so you can avoid them.

But so you can navigate them without losing yourself in the process.

Because the answer isn't to make yourself smaller.

The answer is to understand the game being played—and play it differently.

CHAPTER 5

It's Not Personal

Authority isn't something people grant you. It's something they feel in relation to you.

There's no moment where someone hands you a title or says, "Okay, now you're in charge."

It shows up quietly. In the way the air in the room feels different. In the way conversations shift. In the way you start sensing eyes on you even when no one is saying anything out loud.

It's subtle at first. Easy to second-guess.

You haven't changed. You're still saying the same things. Still showing up the same way. But suddenly, it feels like you're being read differently.

That's the part that messes with your head.

Because when the energy changes, the first place most of us look is inward.

What did I do? What did I say wrong? When did this turn?

But most of the time... it isn't personal.

The comments feel off. The tone changes. The feedback doesn't match what you're actually doing. There's an edge to it that wasn't there before.

Not because you became arrogant—but because authority disrupts the illusion of sameness.

Even in communities built on kindness. Even in spaces that pride themselves on equality.

Authority introduces difference. And difference makes people nervous.

So the story shifts.

Your confidence becomes ego.

Your leadership becomes control.

Your success becomes "trying to own something."

It's easier to moralize discomfort than to sit with it.

And for women especially, it can feel like the same people who were cheering you on—telling you to "fix that crown, queen!"—quietly stop clapping and start whispering.

The side-eye replaces the support.

This is where so many people get stuck.

Because when you're leading with good intentions, the backlash feels confusing. Almost surreal. You start wondering if you misread the moment or misunderstood your role.

But authority has a weight to it. An energy.

Once it's felt, it can't be unfelt.

And not everyone knows how to stay in relationship with you once that shift happens.

So what's actually going on? Why does stepping into authority trigger such a predictable—and painful—response?

It turns out, there's a name for it.

There's a term for what happened in my case—and what happens to countless women building something of their own.

Tall Poppy Syndrome.

The phrase comes from a Roman legend about a king who cut down the tallest poppies in his garden to symbolize removing anyone who stood out too much.

In modern terms, it describes the tendency to criticize, resent, or cut down people who have achieved success.

The research on Tall Poppy Syndrome is extensive, and it shows up everywhere—but it's particularly pronounced when someone from a peer group achieves sudden, visible success, when that success is in an area the group values (like kindness or community), and when the successful person is a woman.

I hit all three.

The Kindness Bucket Brigade grew fast. It was about something everyone valued. And I'm a woman operating in a space where women are supposed to be nurturing and inclusive—not leaders building platforms.

The backlash wasn't about what I did. It was about what my success represented.

It made people uncomfortable. It disrupted the status quo. It forced people to reckon with their own relationship to authority and success.

And rather than sit with that discomfort, it was easier to make me the problem.

Psychologists Henri Tajfel and John Turner developed something called Social Identity Theory in the 1970s.

The basic premise is this: we categorize people as either in-group (like us) or out-group (not like us).

These categorizations happen automatically, subconsciously, and they shape everything from how we interpret someone's actions to how we feel about their success.

When you're a peer—when you're part of the in-group—people give you the benefit of the doubt. They interpret your actions generously. They celebrate your wins because they feel like shared wins.

But the moment you're perceived as having moved into a different category—into authority, into leadership, into a higher status position—you become out-group.

And out-group members are judged more harshly.

The exact same behavior that was endearing when you were a peer becomes threatening when you're an authority.

Confidence becomes arrogance.

Initiative becomes control.

Success becomes proof that you think you're better than everyone else.

This happens even when people consciously want to be supportive. Even when they genuinely like you. Even when they agree with your message.

Because the categorization happens below the level of conscious awareness.

The friend who said it wasn't my thing—that was the one that hurt the most because it came from someone close. Someone I trusted. Someone whose opinion mattered to me.

Looking back, I can see what was really happening.

She was uncomfortable with my success. With the fact that I was getting opportunities and attention. With the shift in our dynamic that neither of us had words for at the time.

But she couldn't say that. Maybe she didn't even consciously realize it.

So instead, she framed it as concern. As honesty. As doing me a favor by telling me I wasn't cut out for this.

This is what psychologists call "Social Correction."

When someone in your group starts to stand out too much, others will often—consciously or unconsciously—try to bring them back down to the group's level.

They do this through criticism, doubt, or subtle undermining disguised as concern.

"I'm just being honest."

"I'm just trying to help."

"I don't want you to get hurt."

What they're really saying is: "You're making me uncomfortable by outgrowing the group."

And when you hear it from a friend, you believe it.

You internalize it. You start to question yourself.

That's why this dynamic is so damaging.

It doesn't just slow you down. It makes you doubt your own instincts, your own capabilities, your own worth.

This is why the backlash feels so confusing and painful.

You didn't do anything wrong. You didn't change. You're still the same person with the same values and intentions.

But other people's relationship to you has changed.

And that change isn't about you—it's about them. It's about their discomfort with the new dynamic. Their anxiety about where they stand in relation to you. Their fear that your success somehow diminishes them.

None of that is rational. None of that is fair. But all of it is real.

When I was getting pushback about The Kindness Bucket Brigade, I internalized it. I thought: *If people are upset, I must be doing something wrong.* What I understand now is that their upset wasn't about my actions. It was about what my authority represented.

It forced people to confront their own relationship with success and authority.

Some people looked at what I built and thought: *If she can do it, maybe I can too.*

Others looked at it and thought: *Who does she think she is?*

Same action. Different interpretation. Based entirely on the viewer's internal relationship with authority.

Here's where it gets really interesting—and kind of dark.

When people feel discomfort but can't name the source, they often turn that discomfort into a moral judgment.

Instead of saying "I feel uncomfortable with your success" (which would require vulnerability and self-awareness), they say "You're doing this wrong."

Instead of "Your authority makes me feel small," they say "You're too self-promotional."

Instead of "I'm threatened by your authority," they say "You've changed."

The discomfort gets reframed as a character flaw in you—rather than an emotional response in them.

It gets dark quickly.

And it's everywhere.

"She's trying to own kindness." (Translation: Her authority in this area makes me uncomfortable.)

"This isn't really her thing." (Translation: I preferred when we were on the same level.)

"She's running a cult." (Translation: The structure and boundaries feel exclusionary to me.)

None of these statements are about objective truth. They're about emotional comfort. But when someone frames their discomfort as a moral failing on your part, it's hard not to internalize it. Especially when it comes from people you respect. People you thought were friends. People whose opinions matter to you.

After The Kindness Bucket Brigade took off, something else started happening. Similar groups started appearing. Same concept. Different name. Different founder.

At first, I was hurt. It felt like people were trying to steal what I'd built.

But what I understand now is that the copycat groups served a psychological function.

They flattened the hierarchy.

If multiple people are doing the same thing, then no one person has authority over it. It becomes democratized again. Communal.

The discomfort of one person having authority in this area gets resolved by making sure everyone has access to the same platform.

It's not actually about the groups themselves. It's about restoring equilibrium.

That's also why imitation shows up after something works, not before. Once an idea gains traction—once it carries trust and authority—duplicating it becomes a way to flatten the field. To bring things back to familiar ground.

If everyone can do it, no one has to acknowledge that you crossed the line first.

When the energy shifts—when people start treating you differently—your first instinct will be to look inward and ask what you did wrong.

Resist that instinct.

Most of the time, the shift isn't about your actions. It's about the role you now occupy in other people's minds.

You've crossed from peer to authority. From in-group to out-group. From relatable to reference point.

That crossing is inevitable if you build anything successful. If you step into any form of leadership. If you claim authority—even accidentally.

The question isn't how to avoid crossing the line.

The question is: how do you operate once you're on the other side?

How do you maintain relationships without shrinking yourself?

How do you hold authority without becoming the villain?

How do you keep building without being destroyed by the scrutiny?

Those are the questions we'll answer in the chapters ahead.

CHAPTER 6

I'm the Problem, It's Me

Sometimes the biggest obstacle to your authority is the word you keep putting in front of it.

I'm a Gen X closeted Swifty. If you have no idea what I'm talking about, the chapter title is from Taylor Swift's song, "Anti-Hero."

For those who aren't Swifties (or closeted ones like me), "Anti-Hero" is a song where Taylor Swift basically turns the mirror on herself and says *I'm the problem here.* It's about self-sabotage, insecurities, and being your own worst critic. The whole hook is her admitting that the thing standing in her way isn't the haters or the critics or the industry—it's her own relationship with herself.

Let me tell you, as I've been writing this book, I've had to turn that same mirror back on myself and really look deep into the moments when I pushed my accomplishments to the back burner and didn't let others acknowledge what I built.

What's ironic is that while I'm writing this book from an authoritative standpoint—because I have done the research and I have lived the experiences—I can also see that I'm perpetually pushing away authority, acknowledgment, praise.

Let me take you back to my next big adventure that started in the summer of 2023.

I had been coaching speakers on how to get paid to speak. These were truly incredible people who had these big life stories. A former NFL player who had become an expert on complex PTSD through his own life experiences. A former 1971 Miss America contestant and one of the original "Breck Girls" who wanted to speak about women aging and societal pressures.

I also had clients who were experts on the homeless crisis, health and wellness, and leadership.

They all had two things in common:

- They had stories with the potential to change lives.

- They were interested in doing a TEDx.

Now, while I had done a TEDx myself, I don't coach speakers on how to apply or get on that stage.

I also know TEDx is strictly about ideas worth spreading. Period. They aren't there to hype your speaking career or to promote your next book. They are about the idea. Not about your business success.

As I had these conversations, I would ask the question, "Okay, what idea would you like to put on the TEDx stage?"

Usually I was met with a shrug and an unsure look.

So I'd follow up with, "What makes you want to do a TEDx?"

That's when the truth would come out.

"Because it would make me look like the expert or the authority."

Ah-ha! That was it.

I knew from doing my own TEDx that it definitely bolstered my career, even if the idea I spoke about had nothing to do with my signature talk around the Complaint Free movement.

I raised my prices.

I added "TEDx Speaker" to my title and bio. Now I was *International and TEDx Speaker, Author.*

Wow. How cool am I?

My next thought was, "Man, I sure wish there was a stage like TEDx—but for stories."

And I continued to daydream about that. It would be an impressive stage, something that looked like a TEDx event.

A theater stage. Yes. Because optics matter.

Then it hit me.

Why don't I create the stage? I love hosting events, and God knows I'm all about the "drama" when it comes to optics.

I let my imagination go wild for a moment.

This would be storytelling. Not a "talk." So it had to *look* different.

A chair. But not any chair. It had to be an armchair. Something soft, dreamy. Maybe blue. Something that screamed storyteller.

Oh, and a rug. Not like the TEDx red dot, but something that defined the area, like a living room. It would be softer, maybe even vintage looking. Gold. Pale yellow.

There should be letters on stage, too. Great lighting. Amazing sound. No hand-held mics. That says low-budget. Instead it would need to be the over-the-ear mics or the ones that clip into your clothing. Hands-free looks more professional.

I started to search my brain for what to call this stage. There had to be a theme. Something specific to what I coach.

And again, like a ton of bricks, it hit me.

WHEN.

This was the question I had been asking for years.

Everyone talks about your "why."

But I was far more fascinated with the "when."

When did everything change?

This question would always take the speaker into a treasure trove of memories—the moments when their life pivoted.

It was how I coached speakers to find stories to use in their talks.

WHEN Talks? Hmm. No. These are stories, not talks.

WHEN Stories? Simple. Descriptive. That was it.

But let's capitalize WHEN so it's like an exclamation mark. WHEN everything changed.

A TEDx-style stage for stories... the moments everything changed.

I wanted to launch this idea in September 2023 at my annual women's event idea. I had a meeting with my marketing coach, and I told her all about this big new idea.

She paused. She thought for a moment, took a deep breath, and said calmly and with love, "I don't get it. You're going to split your audience."

Wait. What? "What do you mean?"

She went on to show me how she'd helped me build a successful coaching business. I was becoming known as The Paid Stage Speaking Coach. People were coming to me to learn how to add a new stream of income through paid speaking.

She went on to say that my ideal client wouldn't benefit from just telling stories, so this new stage wouldn't make sense.

Oof.

I got off the call and honestly, I was royally pissed off. I ranted for a moment to my husband about how she didn't understand what I wanted to do and how I knew this was a great idea.

But that rant didn't last long.

I sat at my office desk. The overhead light was off and only the ring light was shining in front of me.

I felt the tears well up in my eyes.

Dammit.

She was right.

I took a deep breath and tried to blow out all the disappointment filling the air in my lungs.

I'm a run-and-jump-off-the-cliff kind of gal who course corrects as I go, so this was brand new territory for me. For once, I was challenged about my idea before I had the chance to launch it.

I knew I had to ground this idea in reality and make sure it made sense for my ideal client. Which meant there had to be ROI.

It took a year. A year to ask all the questions. Find out what speakers really wanted. Find out what service-based coaches wanted. What held weight? What types of media assets would give them that "expert" feeling or position them as the "authority"?

Because that's what they wanted from TEDx.

WHEN Stories™ became six weeks of story development coaching. Twice a week, I would walk speakers through their "when" moments with a framework I developed. The idea was to lead the audience from when everything changed to the impact they made now in their business.

The other media assets speakers and coaches wanted were podcast placements and books. This made sense because these were assets I knew would showcase them as the go-to experts.

So I made that part of the package. Not only would they tell their WHEN Story on stage, I would create an anthology and a podcast all based around the story they told on stage.

I would also build a YouTube channel, and each story would "premiere" after the stage experience. (Always adding the drama.)

Two weeks before my annual women's event in 2024, I met with my marketing coach again.

I hadn't told her I had been working on this idea. I was too afraid of what she'd say.

"What's your offer for the audience this year?" she asked.

Suddenly, I felt little butterflies in my stomach. I couldn't make eye contact with her when I said:

"Remember that idea I had last year about the stage for stories? Um, yeah. I did what you said and I created a full program of media assets, and I'm calling it WHEN Stories."

As I explained more in depth, I saw her face change from confused to curious. I told her how this would help my ideal clients get booked on more stages and gain more clients.

These were real assets they needed.

There was definitely a plan now for ROI.

I didn't know it then—or didn't have the language for it—but what I had created were authority-building assets.

She nodded and told me she loved the idea.

I seriously got choked up.

At my event that year, I gave my talk from the stage, pitched my offer to the audience about this WHEN Stories idea and…

I filled my first cohort with 12 people. It was beyond my expectations!

That first event was November 2024. The next events followed in March 2025, June 2025, September 2025. All successful. All absolutely more than I could have imagined.

WHEN Stories wasn't just a fleeting idea. It became a business—a movement.

Now, I'm telling you all this for a reason.

After all that work. All the blood, sweat, and tears I put into building this idea—booking discovery calls, setting up the coaching calls, finding the right theaters, the right production team, the right editor for the book, and working through all the "bugs" and building this minute by minute…

On stage after each event, the speakers have all turned to me to thank me with tears in their eyes. They express how this changed their lives.

And I… I think to myself, "But *you're* the one who did it. Why are you thanking *me*? It's *your* story you told. *You* did all the hard work."

I know, I know, you're screaming at me right now… it's the "author" thing all over again.

Yes… it's me. Hi. I'm the problem, it's me.

So let's talk about the elephant in the room.

Did you catch what I just did?

I spent the last several pages telling you how I built WHEN Stories from a daydream into a full business—a coaching program, a stage, an anthology, a podcast, a YouTube channel, four sold-out events in under a year—and then ended it with "but why are you thanking me?"

I literally just walked you through the creation of something that didn't exist before I made it exist... and then dismissed my role in it.

That's not humility. That's the flinch.

It's the same thing I did with "author." The same dance, different stage. I built the thing. I created the framework. I coached every single speaker through their story. I found the theaters, hired the production teams, published the books. I designed that blue armchair moment down to the rug.

And my instinct—even now, even while writing a book about authority—is to hand the credit to someone else and say "I was just the coach."

Just.

There's that word again.

I was *just* there to help. I *just* provided the platform. I *just* asked the right questions.

Do you hear it? Every time I use the word "just," I'm shrinking myself. I'm taking the thing I built and making it smaller so it doesn't feel like I'm claiming too much.

And I know I'm not the only one who does this.

You do it too.

"Oh, I just help people with their finances." No—you're a financial expert who changes people's relationship with money.

"I just share what I've learned." No—you're a thought leader whose knowledge people seek out and pay for.

"I just love what I do." No—you built a business from nothing and people's lives are different because of it.

We "just" ourselves right out of our own authority.

Here's what I've come to understand about why we do this—and I'm speaking specifically to the women reading this book.

We were never taught to claim it.

Think about it. From the time we were little girls, the messaging was clear: be nice, be helpful, be a team player. Share the credit. Don't brag. Don't make it about you. Don't be "too much."

Nobody ever sat us down and said, "When you build something amazing, you're allowed to own that."

Instead, we learned that the "likable" woman is the humble one. The one who deflects compliments. The one who says "oh, it was nothing" when someone acknowledges her work. The one who makes sure everyone else feels comfortable—even if it means making herself invisible.

So we developed a whole vocabulary of deflection.

"I got lucky."

"It was a team effort."

"I had so much help."

"I'm still figuring it out."

"I'm not really an expert, I just have experience."

Every single one of those statements is a woman pressing the "just" button on her own authority.

And here's the messed up part—we don't even realize we're doing it. It's so deeply wired that it feels like modesty. Like good manners. Like being a decent human being.

But it's not modesty. It's erasure.

You're erasing yourself from your own success story.

There's a difference between being humble and being invisible.

Humble is knowing you didn't do it alone and appreciating the people who supported you.

Invisible is pretending you weren't the driving force behind the thing you built.

I can be grateful to every speaker who trusted me with their story and *also* own that I created the stage they stood on. Those two things aren't in conflict.

But for years, I acted like they were. Like acknowledging my role somehow took away from theirs. Like owning my authority meant I was saying their courage didn't matter.

It doesn't work that way.

Their bravery on that stage and my authority in building it can both be true at the same time.

So why am I telling you all of this now?

Because if you've read this far, I know something about you.

You've built something. Maybe it's a business. Maybe it's a body of expertise. Maybe it's a reputation, a community, a career that you've poured yourself into for years.

And there's a very good chance you're standing in the middle of what you've built, looking around at everything you created, and still thinking... "but I'm not really an authority."

Yes, you are.

You're just afraid to say it out loud.

And I get it. I'm literally writing the book on this, and I still catch myself flinching.

But here's what I know for sure: the invisible line doesn't just get drawn by other people.

Sometimes we draw it on ourselves.

Every time we say "just." Every time we deflect a compliment. Every time we hand our credit to someone else because owning it feels like too much.

We cross back over that line—the one we worked so hard to get to the other side of—and we put ourselves right back where we started.

And now that we can see it—really see it—we can stop doing it.

CHAPTER 7

The Golden Ticket

Access lowers perceived value. Distance creates it.

"Do you know the quickest way to become an expert?"

There was an anticipatory pause from all of us backstage.

"A plane ticket."

Everyone laughed. The joke landed because it struck a chord of truth for each of us.

This happened backstage at a speaking competition. We were talking about getting booked to speak and how no events within driving distance seemed willing to pay us. That's when I brought up proximity.

I explained my theory that showing up more was actually hurting most of us.

In networking groups. In masterminds. In our communities.

I remembered something Will Bowen once mentioned to me about a very well-known speaker.

He said it didn't matter who you were—you didn't get access to him unless you were a paying client. He didn't network or schmooze with other speakers.

He designed it that way intentionally.

Because he understood something most people resist accepting.

Access lowers perceived value.

At the time, I remember thinking, *What a douche. That's a terrible way to do business.*

Now?

I'm not so sure.

As speakers and entrepreneurs, we're taught that the answer is always more involvement. More visibility. More presence. More availability.

So that's what we do.

We join the groups. Attend the events. Say yes to coffee chats. Show up early. Stay late.

And at first, it feels right. Helpful. Generous. Connected.

But slowly, something starts to shift.

The more familiar you become, the less weight your words seem to carry.

I noticed it happening to me. I saw it happening to others in the same rooms—people with real experience, real insight, real results.

And if I'm honest, I was just as guilty of it as everyone else.

After the pandemic, I started coaching speakers on how to get paid to speak.

Many of them couldn't understand why organizations would pay someone from the outside.

So I'd ask them to think back to their old jobs.

You hear the same messages over and over from the boss, usually wrapped in some version of a tired pep talk.

"Okay team, let's be more productive, talk a little less, stop complaining, and love our jobs!"

Well... not exactly like that. But you get the idea.

It's the same voice. The same delivery. The same proximity.

Eventually, everyone tunes it out.

Then the company hosts an event. Maybe a retreat. A team-building day. And they bring in a speaker.

Someone entertaining. Funny. Someone with stories. Someone new.

They say the exact same things—work a little harder, communicate better, solve problems, appreciate the team you work with.

But this time?

Everyone is listening.

Nothing about the message changed.

Only the distance.

You were too close to the boss.

The speaker who flew in wasn't.

The plane ticket didn't make them smarter. It made them separate.

And separation created value.

That's when the joke stopped being funny and started being uncomfortable.

Because it wasn't really about expertise.

It was about proximity.

At some point, without realizing it, being seen turns into being known. People don't just recognize you—they have access to you. They know your backstory. They've watched your journey unfold in real time.

And while connection is powerful, over-familiarity has a cost.

You don't notice the moment it happens. There's no announcement. No warning sign.

You just start feeling it.

The ignored suggestion. The passed-over opportunity. The polite nod instead of the invitation.

You become "one of us."

And "one of us" rarely gets brought in from the outside.

They want someone else.

Someone unfamiliar. Someone untouched by the dynamics. Someone who doesn't live in their world.

It's the same reason people feel oddly important when they went to high school with someone who later becomes famous.

They once shared space. Proximity creates a sense of connection—even if they passed each other in the hallway a thousand times and never once spoke.

This past September, my husband and I went to Door County, Wisconsin, for a day trip to celebrate our 11-year wedding anniversary. We booked a lighthouse trolley tour.

The tour was excellent. Our driver was entertaining, funny, and incredibly knowledgeable.

When we stopped for lunch, Brian and I grabbed our prepared meals and sat at an empty picnic table. About halfway through our sandwiches, the trolley driver came over and asked if he could sit with us.

Of course, we struck up a conversation.

We talked about all sorts of things in that short time, and at one point music came up. My husband mentioned my win at the Hollywood Independent Music Awards that summer for my song, "She Was Here."

The driver shared that his daughter-in-law was an up-and-coming artist, so I followed her on social media.

She had a great voice. A great presence. A lot of potential.

About six months later, I was scrolling Facebook when I saw news stations covering a Wisconsin woman who had just received a golden ticket to Hollywood on American Idol.

I clicked the article.

Her face looked familiar.

Then I saw her name.

It was the trolley driver's daughter-in-law.

And instantly, I thought, *Wow. I know her!*

No, I don't.

I've never met her. We've never spoken. But because I had proximity to someone connected to her, my brain created a sense of closeness.

That's proximity.

It creates perceived access—even when none exists.

And perceived access quietly changes how we value people.

Most entrepreneurs never realize when they've crossed that invisible line.

They just wake up one day wondering why they're everywhere... yet somehow no longer being invited in.

I was still showing up and doing everything I was told to do—but whatever used to work wasn't working anymore.

And then there was the coaching call that changed everything.

The people pleaser in me has always made it hard to set boundaries. So when I found myself an hour over the time allotted for a 45-minute free coaching call I'd offered, I was frustrated. I was trying to get a word in edgewise and find a tactful way to end the call.

And then she said it.

"Wendy, you have been so helpful! I cannot thank you enough. I just paid thousands of dollars to [big name coach] and this session with you helped me more than they have."

What. The. Fuck.

And yes—she was still actively coaching with them. Still paying them. Thousands of dollars.

Sure wish she would have told me that at the beginning of the call.

Here I was thinking I was "doing the right thing" by really listening, providing my expertise, and answering her questions. Under-promise and over-deliver, like "they" tell you to do.

Only to learn I had just spent an hour and forty-five minutes helping someone for free—someone who was literally paying someone else thousands of dollars for the same thing.

And do you know WHY that happened?

It wasn't because I sent out an email offering a free 45-minute coaching call. That part was fine.

It happened because she had been on my email list for years. She came to every free mastermind. Every free workshop. Every *free* thing that I offered.

She had unlimited access to me. She knew she could get my expertise anytime she wanted, for *nothing*.

So why would she pay me?

She paid the other coach—the one with distance, the one she didn't have casual access to, the one who wasn't showing up in her inbox every week with another free offer.

Not because that coach was better. I proved that on the call.

Because that coach had separation. And separation created value.

Remember in the last chapter when I talked about the word "just"? How we use it to shrink ourselves and our authority?

This is what "just" looks like in practice.

I was "just" being helpful. I was "just" going the extra mile. I was "just" doing what good coaches do.

And every "just" cost me. Not just the hour and forty-five minutes. It cost me the authority I'd earned—because I had trained her and everyone like her to expect my expertise for free.

My generosity wasn't generosity. It was over-accessibility disguised as good business.

And it was eroding the very authority I was trying to build.

The "plane ticket" joke is funny because it's true.

Being from out of town automatically increases your perceived value—even if your actual expertise is identical to someone local.

This isn't fair. It's not rational. But it is predictable.

Organizations will pay thousands of dollars to fly someone in, put them up in a hotel, and pay their speaking fee—while ignoring the equally qualified speaker who lives twenty minutes away.

Why?

Because the local speaker is too accessible. Too familiar. Too "one of us."

The speaker from out of town carries an implicit endorsement: if they're worth flying in, they must be worth listening to.

This is what proximity does. It rewards scarcity over availability.

So what's the answer?

Do you become inaccessible? Hide from your community? Turn into that speaker Will told me about who doesn't network with anyone?

Not exactly.

The answer is strategic distance—or "proximity by design," as I like to call it.

Proximity by design means being intentional about when, where, and how you make yourself available. It means understanding that your time, your presence, and your expertise have value—and that value is partly determined by scarcity.

It's the difference between building genuine relationships and over-saturating your market. Between showing up where it matters and showing up everywhere because you're afraid to miss something.

It means you don't attend every networking event—you choose the ones that align with your goals. You don't say yes to every coffee chat—you protect your time and energy for high-value connections. You don't give away all your expertise for free—you create clear boundaries between what's freely available and what requires investment. You don't make yourself endlessly available—you create containers for access. Paid programs. Scheduled calls. Office hours.

This isn't about being a douche. It's about being strategic.

Because the truth is: the more accessible you are, the less valuable you appear.

And the less valuable you appear, the harder it is to claim the authority you've earned.

Here's what I wish someone had told me before that coaching call. Before the years of free workshops and coffee chats and showing up everywhere for everyone.

Proximity is a tool—not a strategy.

In the early stages of building authority, proximity helps. People need to know you, trust you, see you as accessible.

But there's a tipping point where proximity stops building authority and starts eroding it. Where your generosity trains people to take instead of invest. Where your availability makes you invisible instead of valuable.

That tipping point—the invisible line—is different for everyone. When you're visible everywhere and opportunities aren't increasing, when people seek your advice freely but won't pay for your expertise, when your calendar is full of coffee chats but not clients, when you feel burned out from being so available but not valued—you've crossed it.

And once you see it, you can't unsee it.

The plane ticket isn't just about geography.

It's about separation.

And sometimes, the most powerful thing you can do for your authority is to create space between yourself and everyone else.

CHAPTER 8

Helpful But Not Hirable

The visibility that builds connection rarely builds revenue.

I had quit my 20-year career at the hospital in September 2017.

I had reached the point where I was starting to get a few speaking opportunities, but working full time was limiting which gigs I could actually take. I loved sharing the Complaint Free message, and I realized pretty quickly that I loved being on stage.

Around that time, a friend kept inviting me to a networking group event. She mentioned it more than once, and every time I brushed it off.

I had never networked before and, honestly, I didn't understand the point of it at all.

With some persistence, she finally got a "fine, I'll go" out of me.

After an hour-and-forty-minute drive, I arrived. There were already quite a few women in the room. Many of them came over right away, recognizing I was a new face. They said hello, welcomed me, and introduced themselves.

That helped, because I was nervous.

I've always felt socially awkward, and I truly had no idea what to expect.

The meeting started. After the managing director's introduction, we were told we'd each give a 60-second introduction—who we were and what we did.

Suddenly, my mind went completely blank.

What do I say? What am I supposed to say?

Instant panic.

My internal voice chimed in immediately: *Don't say something stupid.*

One by one, each woman stood up and gave her elevator introduction. Most sounded something like this:

"Hi, I'm _________. My business is _________. I help _________ do _________ so they can _________."

Okay. Almost your turn. Don't stumble over your words.

When it was my turn, I stood up.

"Hi. I'm Wendy Babcock. I'm a Certified Complaint Free Speaker. I just started last year... and I don't know what else to say."

That was basically it.

Ugh. I sounded so dumb.

But as the meeting went on, I listened.

I listened to women talk about their businesses, their struggles, their upcoming events, and the ways they supported one another.

And I had this sudden realization.

They were just like me.

Maybe they weren't speakers, but they were building businesses on their own. Figuring things out as they went. Taking risks. Putting themselves out there.

They were just like me.

And then it hit me.

This is why people network.

By the end of the meeting, I was all in. I joined for a full year on the spot.

I went to as many meetings as I could.

Then I joined another group.

And then another.

Because that's what you're told to do.

Build relationships. Expand your circle. Be visible. Get in the room.

So I did.

More 60-second introductions. More early mornings and late nights. More driving. More calendars filling up.

Soon, my weeks were stacked with one-on-one Zoom calls. Coffee chats. "Let's connect" conversations.

I introduced one woman to another. Referred this person to that person. Made mental notes about who did what so I could play matchmaker.

I was helpful. I was generous. I was involved.

And it felt good.

Not just productive—it felt meaningful.

I was building genuine relationships. I liked these women. I wanted to help them succeed. But there was something else happening underneath all that generosity. Something I didn't recognize at the time.

I was training people to expect my expertise for free.

The conversations were warm. Encouraging. Supportive. Women would approach me after meetings.

"Can I pick your brain about speaking?"

"Do you have time for a quick coffee? I'd love your thoughts on my business."

"Would you mind looking at my presentation and giving me feedback?"

And I'd say yes.

Every time.

Because I wanted to be helpful. Because that's what you do in a community. Because saying no felt selfish.

But here's what I didn't understand then:

Every time I gave away my expertise for free, I reinforced the idea that my expertise wasn't valuable enough to pay for.

I started hearing the same frustrations from the women around me.

Different voices. Same confusion.

"They know what I do."

"I'm always helping everyone else."

"They come to me for advice, but no one wants to pay me."

And I'd nod along, completely missing the irony.

Because I was doing the exact same thing.

Giving away the very expertise I was trying to build a business around.

But when it came to actual paying clients?

Crickets.

That's when I realized: I had built a reputation for being helpful, but not for being hirable.

If you've been following the thread through this book, you can probably see the pattern forming.

In the last chapter, I told you about the coaching call where I spent an hour and forty-five minutes giving free advice to a woman who was paying someone else thousands of dollars. That was the moment I saw the cost of over-accessibility.

But this—the networking years—this was the slow, invisible buildup to that moment.

I wasn't just over-accessible on one phone call. I had spent years making myself endlessly available. Years of coffee chats and brain-picking sessions and free feedback. Years of being the most helpful person in the room.

And all of it—every generous act, every "of course I have time," every "happy to help"—was quietly eroding the authority I was trying to build.

Remember what proximity does? It lowers perceived value.

I wasn't just close to these women. I was *too* close. Too available. Too free.

They didn't see me as the expert they'd hire.

They saw me as the friend they'd call.

And the friend never gets the contract.

Now here's where this story gets uncomfortable.

Because while I was busy being helpful but not hirable, I was also lying.

Not maliciously. Not intentionally.

But I was lying all the same.

Over and over I repeated the same thing to my clients: You don't need a big following, a TEDx, a book, or any fancy visibility to get booked and paid to speak.

I mean, I didn't have any of that when I started, so this is what I preached.

At the beginning of my speaking career, I learned how to cold email effectively and how to get hired to speak. It was a numbers game. I was sending 50+ emails a week and booking maybe one gig a month. It was exhausting, but it paid the bills.

I didn't see the value of social media. At most, I knew I had to keep my profiles upbeat and professional. I didn't view them as a reason anyone would book me to speak at their event.

It was a grind. But I was making it work.

Then 2020 happened.

I was booked to speak at Lambeau Field in Green Bay that May. To say I was devastated when it was cancelled is an understatement.

Gigs postponed one after another, then cancelled one after another. Some went virtual, but I wasn't feeling it—cameras off, tech glitchy, zero energy.

I floundered for a while trying to find something—anything—to bring money in. I started a networking business, ran some summits, tried to make the virtual thing work.

Nothing stuck.

Then in 2021, I met a marketing strategist, Alexis, who changed everything.

When I told her I felt like I'd lost my way and didn't know what I "wanted to be when I grow up," she asked me one question:

"What do people come to you for advice about?"

Easy. People asked me how I got paid to speak. I knew how to build a great signature talk and how to add stories to make it inspiring and entertaining.

With that, I had a coaching business in the making. I would become The Paid Stage Speaking Coach.

After working with a client who was struggling to add stories to his talk, my advice was to look for those "when moments"—the moments when everything changed.

This became my go-to advice for finding stories. Not the why—the *when*.

I was working on crafting a new signature talk and decided to take my own advice. I did a brainstorming session of when moments.

I created a timeline with one horizontal line on my paper. I quickly wrote down pivotal moments, careful not to overthink them.

Wrote first book.

Wrote second book.

Did my TEDx.

I stopped.

Blinked at the paper.

Read it again.

Oh shit.

I've been wrong this whole time.

I've been teaching people to do it the hard way—the cold email grind, the numbers game, the exhausting hustle—while I took a different path and pretended I didn't.

Those moments—the books and the TEDx—did change everything.

I did feel more confident.

I did gain followers.

I did increase my keynote pricing.

I did get taken more seriously.

I did get invited to stages I never would have been considered for before.

So that begged the question: did I need those things to be successful?

No.

But did they majorly help?

Absolutely.

And I'd been telling people they didn't matter.

It made me recalibrate everything I was teaching.

It made me realize I'd completely stepped over another invisible line without even recognizing it.

It made me realize I had lied—that those things absolutely do get you booked and paid more.

Not because they make you a better speaker.

But because they change how people perceive you.

They signal authority in a way that cold emails never will.

They create credibility that's hard to build any other way.

They open doors that hustle alone can't open.

And that's when something clicked—something I couldn't quite name at the time but can now.

There was a word for what those assets did. A word the entire online business world was obsessed with.

Visibility.

But the more I thought about it, the more I realized it wasn't that simple. Because I'd been "visible" for years. I was visible at every networking meeting. I was visible on every coffee chat. I was visible in every Facebook group, every mastermind, every free workshop I hosted.

I was one of the most visible people in my circles.

And it wasn't working.

So either visibility was a lie... or there was more than one kind.

It turns out, it was the second one. And understanding the difference between the two would change everything about how I built my business.

But before I explain what I mean, I need to tell you about the night I won a music award in Hollywood. Because that story—and what happened a few months later—is what finally made the distinction click.

CHAPTER 9

And the Winner Is

Not all visibility is created equal.

"The winner is... Wendy Babcock!"

In that moment, I chucked my phone at my husband. My pulse must have been over 200. I could feel my body shaking.

And I took off.

Just go! Go!

That's all I could think. *Run, Forrest, run!*

I knew being in the upper balcony it was going to be a sprint to get to the stage. With my hands cupped over my mouth and nose in absolute shock, I ran down two flights of stairs, stopping anyone who looked like a staff member.

"How do I get down there? I just won!"

They pointed me in the right direction.

I weaved my way through the crowd and made it into the main theater, then up to the stage.

I was in Hollywood at the famous Avalon Theater, accepting the award for my song "She Was Here" in the Message Song / Social Impact category.

This was a moment I could have never predicted.

My social media blew up that week. My engagement was through the roof.

When I came off the red carpet, I recorded a quick video talking about how the founder of the Hollywood Independent Music Awards knew who I was and the name of my song. I was in utter disbelief. There had to be a couple hundred entries across all the different categories.

In hindsight, I realized he obviously knew I was the winner of my category. In fact, other moments played back in slow motion—*oh! That's why they made sure I was interviewed. That's why they shouted my name across the room at each other like I was someone important.*

When I got back to my hotel room after the awards, I recorded another video thanking everyone for their support and all the interaction following my journey to Hollywood. It was so nice to post about the whole experience and have so many people cheering me on.

What a rush!

Then a few months later—

"It is a pleasure to announce that the Small Business of the Year award goes to... Wendy Babcock!"

What?!

Again, absolute shock.

A community I'm a member of called The Small Business Owners Community held their yearly awards at their conference, and I was nominated for Small Business of the Year alongside businesses—friends—that certainly deserved it more than me. Or so I thought.

Was this too much?

Yes, this went through my head as I saw comments like:

"Boy, you're having quite the year!"

"Wow! Another award?! Congratulations!"

All good intentions. So much amazing support.

But something inside me shrunk.

Is this too much?

Am I too much?

Will people think I'm "too big for my britches" now?

Words played through my mind that I'd heard before: "Don't forget about all us little people."

What was it about success that made other people categorize themselves as "little people?" I often wondered this. Successful people are just… people.

Now, to be fair, I was the only one in this scenario questioning whether people were secretly rolling their eyes about these two big wins back to back.

Here's what I didn't understand then: both awards were earned. Both were legitimate. Both represented real accomplishment.

So why did one feel like celebration and the other feel like… exposure?

The difference wasn't in the awards themselves.

It was in *who was watching.*

In Hollywood, I was surrounded by strangers. People who didn't know my story, didn't know my struggles, didn't know the version of me who started writing songs at age 11, who met my cowriter on Myspace back in 2007, and all the songs we shopped around Nashville for years with no luck.

They only saw the winner on stage.

There was distance. Separation. No history. No context.

Just the moment.

And in that moment, I could be whoever I wanted to be. I could celebrate without worrying about how it looked. I could post on social media without second-guessing whether I was "too much."

Because none of those people knew me before I crossed the line.

But the local award?

That was different.

These were people who *did* know me. People who'd seen me at networking events every month. People who'd grabbed coffee with me. People who knew I was "one of them"—another entrepreneur just trying to figure it out.

We were peers.

The Hollywood award let me exist on the other side of the line with an audience that had only ever known me there.

The local award forced me to cross the line in front of people who remembered all my struggles.

That's what made me shrink.

Not the accomplishment itself. Not the recognition.

The proximity.

Because here's the truth I didn't want to admit: I wasn't afraid of success.

I was afraid of being seen succeeding by people who knew me when I was still struggling.

I was afraid they'd think I thought I was better than them.

I was afraid of the invisible line between "You go, girl!" and "Who does she think she is?"

And that fear—that specific, proximity-based fear—is what kept me from fully celebrating something I'd legitimately earned.

But sitting with those two experiences side by side taught me something I don't think I could have learned any other way.

Both awards made me visible. Both put my name and face in front of people. Both generated social media engagement and congratulations and all the things you'd expect from a "visibility win."

But they felt completely different. And they *functioned* completely differently.

The Hollywood award didn't just make me visible—it made me credible to a new audience. People who had no idea who I was now associated me with an accomplishment. I wasn't "Wendy from the networking group." I was "an award-winning songwriter." That visibility *meant* something. It carried weight.

The local award made me visible too—but to an audience that already knew me. They were happy for me, sure. But it didn't change how they perceived me. I was still Wendy. Still the woman they'd had coffee with. Still "one of us."

Same accomplishment. Same award. Different impact.

And that's when I started to realize that visibility isn't one thing.

It's two.

When most people talk about "getting visible," they're lumping two completely different things into one vague concept.

But the type of visibility you build—or accidentally fall into—determines everything about how your business grows, how people perceive you, and whether your success feels sustainable or exhausting.

The first type is what I call ego-centric visibility. This is visibility that's about *you being seen.* It's built around the idea that if enough people know your name, know your face, know you exist, opportunities will follow.

It's not inherently bad or wrong. But it looks like posting constantly on social media to stay top of mind. Buying a Times Square billboard so you can say you were on a Times Square billboard. Purchasing awards or "bestseller" status. Chasing follower counts. Paying to be featured on magazine covers. Being everywhere, all the time, because you're afraid people will forget you.

The driving force behind ego-centric visibility is fear of irrelevance. If you're not constantly visible, you think people will forget you exist. So you keep showing up, keep posting, keep finding new ways to put your name in front of people.

It's exhausting.

And if you're feeling called out right now, don't worry—I'm calling myself out too.

Here's the question that changed how I think about all of it: Do you want to look famous to your neighbors, or be the authority that event planners and clients can't ignore?

Here's the thing: ego-centric visibility *works*—to a point. People do see you. They do know your name. You do get recognized. But recognition doesn't always translate to revenue. Or respect. Or the kind of opportunities that actually move your business forward.

The second type is what I call authority-based visibility. This is visibility that's about *what you've built or earned.* It's not about being seen—it's about being valued for something specific.

It looks like being invited to speak at an industry conference because of your expertise. Earning an award through competition or merit. Getting featured in media because a journalist sought you out. Publishing a book based on your knowledge. Being referenced or cited by others in your field. Creating work that speaks for itself.

The driving force behind authority-based visibility is contribution. You're visible because you've done something noteworthy, created something valuable, or solved a problem others couldn't.

Authority-based visibility is slower to build. But it compounds. Once you have it, it works for you even when you're not actively maintaining it. It's the difference between running on a hamster wheel and building a flywheel.

The simplest way I can break it down is this:

Ego-centric visibility asks: *How can I get more people to see me?*

Authority-based visibility asks: *What can I create or accomplish that's worth being seen for?*

One is about attention. The other is about impact.

One requires constant feeding. The other builds momentum.

One makes you feel like you're running to keep up. The other makes you feel like you're building something that lasts.

Now here's what makes this complicated—and why the two-award experience mattered so much.

Both of my awards were authority-based. I didn't buy them. I didn't pay to be nominated. I earned them through actual work.

So why did one feel empowering and the other feel threatening?

Because authority-based visibility doesn't eliminate the invisible line. It just changes how you experience it.

In Hollywood, I was experiencing authority-based visibility with a *distant audience.* They didn't know me before. The line was already crossed in their perception. I was always "the winner on stage" to them.

In my local community, I was experiencing authority-based visibility with a *close audience.* They knew me before. They watched me cross the line. And that proximity amplified every anxiety I had about being "too much."

This is the part the visibility conversation almost never addresses: it's not just about *which type* of visibility you build. It's also about *who sees you* when you build it.

And I want to be clear about something—ego-centric visibility isn't "wrong" or "bad." There are times when it makes sense. But you have to know what you're doing and why.

Because some visibility opportunities sit right in the middle, and the difference comes down to what you're actually contributing.

Take magazine features, for example. Paying for a photo on a magazine cover? That's ego-centric—you're just putting your face there. Paying to contribute an expert article or a thought leadership piece? That's authority-based—you're sharing knowledge, even if you paid for placement.

The question isn't always, "Did I pay for this?" Sometimes it's, "Am I contributing value, or just buying space?"

Here's a test I use now, and I think it's worth sharing.

You're offered the chance to nominate yourself for an award. You pay the organization and are guaranteed a "win" or some kind of "acknowledgment" for this investment.

Now imagine: if you were to post the award, get tons of interactions and congratulations, and then announce that you paid for that opportunity—how would your audience respond?

Would they say, "What a cool opportunity!"?

Or would they feel misled that it wasn't an earned award?

That's your litmus test.

If your audience would celebrate the strategy, it might be a smart ego-centric visibility play. If they'd lose trust in your credibility, that's not an opportunity—it's a risk.

Most entrepreneurs and speakers I work with are being sold ego-centric tactics while trying to build authority-based businesses. They're buying billboards and fake bestseller lists and paid magazine covers, and then wondering why none of it translates into real clients, real stages, or real respect.

It's not that they're doing visibility wrong.

It's that they're doing the wrong *kind* of visibility for what they're trying to build.

And that mismatch—that gap between the visibility you're chasing and the authority you actually need—is why so much of the visibility advice out there feels like complete bullshit.

Because it is.

At least, the version most people are being sold.

What I know now—what I wish I'd known during all those networking years, all those coffee chats, all those free workshops—is that real visibility isn't about being visible.

It's about being seen *for something that matters.*

And the only way to build that kind of visibility is to first build the authority behind it.

That's what the books did for me. That's what the TEDx did. That's what WHEN Stories does for the speakers I work with. Not because those things make you more visible—although they do—but because they give people a reason to pay attention.

Authority first. Visibility second.

Get that order wrong, and you'll spend years being the most visible person in the room—who nobody hires.

CHAPTER 10

Shhh... Don't Tell Anyone

The invisible line doesn't just show up when you grow. It shows up when you watch someone else grow too.

Sometimes it's not what people say as much as how the energy changes when you walk in the room.

Women have an intuition, a radar about who feels threatened by them. Maybe not all women, but the ones I know definitely do. It's one of those moments you can't prove but you inherently feel.

This is where the invisible line really stems from. I've talked about owning your authority, being intentional with proximity, and knowing which visibility is helping you or hurting you. Each of those carries its own invisible line.

But when I decided to write this book, I realized the REAL invisible line shows up when you grow. When you start to find success. When you're noticed. When the visibility works.

Suddenly, you're told your name is buzzing. So-and-so mentioned your business. Your name is in the room before you are.

It's an invisible line because everything associated with it is also invisible. No one usually comes out and tells you they think you're getting too big for your britches, but you can tell that's what they're thinking. It might be a tone they use. It might be the slight eye roll you notice. Maybe it's how someone tries to hint to you that your name came up in a not-so-nice way.

The parts that aren't invisible are the gossip that makes its way back to you.

She charges too much.

Anyone can do that, what makes her so special?

I could do that.

When those things get back to you or you *feel* them in the room with you, that's when you know.

You crossed the invisible line.

And man, as much as I hate to say this—women sure can be bitches.

They'll rip you apart behind your back.

They'll make snide comments about something you're passionate about.

They'll talk mad shit to their networks about you.

And the worst part? People who don't even know you will suddenly have an opinion, too. Because someone was intimidated by your success and needed to spread that discomfort around.

It's not fair.

And we all do it.

Don't shake your head no. We ALL do it, at some level.

Maybe you're not the woman who is whispering in the hallway at a networking event, but you might be rolling your eyes when you scroll social media and see another "win" for someone you follow.

Oh good lord, another award?

Really? Another media interview? She must be paying for that.

Must be nice to have that kind of time.

We all do it. Internally or externally.

This is what has to change. And I'm not sitting up here on my high horse shaking my finger at you. I'm turning the mirror on myself in this moment. Because I know I've been intimidated by other women in business.

I don't know if it's jealousy, authority anxiety, or intimidation. But it's... something.

And until we name that something, we keep the cycle going. We keep drawing invisible lines around other women's success. And then we're shocked—shocked—when someone draws one around ours.

As I've been telling women I'm close to about this phenomenon of the invisible line—how when your business starts gaining real momentum, people suddenly start falling off like flies—I get the same response every time.

"Oh my God! That's happening to me right now!"

Or: "Holy shit! Yes! Finally someone gets it!"

Every. Single. Time.

And what breaks my heart is the relief in their voices. Like they've been carrying this alone. Like they thought they were the only ones feeling the shift, noticing the distance, absorbing the whispers.

They weren't crazy. They weren't being too sensitive. They weren't imagining it.

They convinced themselves they did something wrong.

They crossed the invisible line. And they paid for it with relationships they thought were safe.

So here's what I want to do with you right now. And I'm warning you—this part is going to be uncomfortable.

I want you to turn the mirror on yourself.

Not the version of you who's been hurt by someone else's reaction to your success. We've spent the whole book talking about that. You see that clearly now. You have the language for it. Authority, proximity, visibility—you get it.

I want you to look at the other version of you. The one who's on the other side of someone else's invisible line.

Because she's there. She exists. And she's the key to breaking this whole cycle.

Think about the last time you saw another woman post a big win on social media.

Not a close friend. Not someone you're genuinely rooting for. I mean a woman in your space, in your industry, maybe someone you loosely know. She posts about a major client she landed. A stage she booked. An award she won. A revenue milestone she hit.

What was your first reaction?

Not the one you typed in the comments. Not the "Congratulations!" with the heart emoji.

The first one. The *real* one. The one that flickered through your mind before you had a chance to edit it.

Was it genuine happiness for her?

Or was it something else?

Maybe a quick flash of *must be nice.* Maybe a sting of comparison. Maybe a thought you'd never say out loud—*what makes her so special?*

If something uncomfortable just surfaced, stay with it for a second. Don't push it away. Don't shame yourself for it.

That reaction? That flicker? That's the invisible line—and you just drew it around her.

Here's what I've learned about that flicker: it's never actually about the other woman.

It's about what her success is reflecting back to you about where you are.

When someone in your space wins, it holds up a mirror—whether you asked for one or not. And what you see in that mirror isn't her accomplishment. It's the gap between where she is and where you think you should be.

That's what stings. Not her win. Your gap.

And because that gap is painful and we don't have great language for it, we do what humans have always done with discomfort we can't name. We moralize it. We make it about her.

She's probably exaggerating.

She must have connections I don't have.

I bet she's not as successful as she's making it look.

Sound familiar? It should. It's the same moralization of discomfort we talked about in Chapter 5—just from the other side of the line.

So the next time you feel that reaction rising up—the eye roll, the scroll past someone's win without engaging, the "good for her" that doesn't quite land as genuine—I want you to stop.

Don't judge yourself. Just ask yourself one question:

What is her success bringing up in me right now?

Not what did she do. Not whether she deserves it. Not how she got there.

What is it bringing up in *you*?

Because the answer to that question is never about her. It's about something you want, something you're afraid of, or something you haven't given yourself permission to pursue yet.

Maybe her stage win reminds you that you've been sitting on your own talk for two years.

Maybe her book launch reminds you that you keep saying "someday" about yours.

Maybe her revenue post reminds you that you're still undercharging because you're afraid to claim your own value.

Her win isn't your loss. Her win is your mirror.

And what you do with what you see in that mirror determines whether you stay stuck on your side of the invisible line or finally cross it yourself.

Now flip it.

Think about a time you felt the temperature change. When someone you trusted started pulling away. When the group chat got quieter after your big announcement. When a friend's tone shifted, and you couldn't quite put your finger on why.

Ask yourself: did you do something wrong?

Or did you just grow?

Because odds are, you didn't change who you were. You changed what you represented. And someone on the other side of your invisible line had that same flicker—that same mirror moment—and instead of sitting with what it brought up for them, they made it about you.

She's changed.

She thinks she's better than us.

She charges too much.

That wasn't about you. That was about their gap. Their discomfort. Their invisible line.

You just happened to be on the other side of it.

This is the part of the book where I need you to hold two things at the same time.

You have been hurt by this dynamic. That's real. That pain is real. The friendships that changed, the whispers, the slow fade of people you thought were your people—all of that happened and it mattered.

And you have also been the one doing it to someone else. Maybe not with gossip. Maybe not with whispers. But with an eye roll. A scroll. A thought you'd never say out loud. A distance you created because someone's success made you uncomfortable.

Both of those things are true. And both of those things are part of the invisible line.

The only way to stop the cycle is to recognize yourself on both sides of it.

When someone else grows, let them. Feel the flicker. Name what it brings up. And then ask yourself what it's telling you about what *you* want.

When you grow, let yourself. Feel the shift around you. Name what's happening. And stop blaming yourself for other people's discomfort.

The invisible line will always be there. People will always react when you cross it. And you'll always feel something when you watch someone else cross theirs.

But now you see it. You have the language for it. And seeing it—really *seeing* it—changes everything.

Because the woman who understands the invisible line doesn't stop growing.

She just stops being surprised when the room gets quiet.

And she stops being the reason someone else's room gets quiet too.

PART TWO
NAVIGATING THE INVISIBLE LINE

CHAPTER 11

Grow or Show

You need people who see everything. And you need people who only see what matters.

I made a lot of realizations when I started digging deep to write this book.

It wasn't easy. I had to really look at myself, my business, and the rooms I put myself in. I had to stop blaming the dynamics and start examining my own choices—where I was showing up, how I was showing up, and who I was showing up for.

And when I did that, I started to see the patterns.

Every community I joined followed the same arc. I'd be excited to find a new group. I'd meet new people. We'd get to know each other, grow together, share wins and losses, learn from each other's mistakes. It was energizing. It felt like home.

Then something would shift.

I'd start feeling like I was too well known in the room. Not taken seriously the way I once was. Passed over for opportunities I knew I was qualified for. I was the go-to speaking expert in these circles—the person everyone came to with questions about getting on stages—and yet I wasn't being put on stages myself.

They knew too much about me. They'd watched me figure things out in real time. They'd seen the messy middle—the pivot to the networking company during the pandemic, the pivot back to speaking, the pivot into coaching. They'd been on the ride with me through all of it.

And that ride—as much as I loved them for being on it—cost me my authority in their eyes.

Not because they were bad people. Not because they didn't respect me.

Because they saw too much. And when people see too much, they stop seeing you as the expert. They see you as the person who was just figuring it out alongside them last Tuesday.

That's proximity doing what proximity does.

When I finally understood what was happening, I didn't feel angry. I felt relieved.

I was expecting these groups—the ones where I'd been vulnerable, messy, uncertain, and real—to also be the groups that hired me, referred me, and treated me like the authority I'd become.

But that's not how it works.

The people who watched you grow rarely see you as the expert. They see you as the woman who used to be right where they are. And no amount of success changes that perception—because proximity has already done its work.

So I stopped fighting it. And I gave it a name.

These were my GROW groups.

A GROW group is exactly what it sounds like—a group you grow with.

These are the people who see everything. Your wins and your losses. Your confidence and your doubt. The launches that flopped and the ideas that didn't land. The moments you cried at your desk and the moments you almost quit.

They know the real you. The unfiltered, behind-the-scenes, sometimes-a-mess you.

And that's exactly what makes them valuable.

Because you need people like that. You need a room where you can say "I have no idea what I'm doing right now" and nobody loses faith in you. You need friends who will tell you your pricing page is confusing, your last email was too long, or your new idea needs more work. You need the people who will celebrate your wins without jealousy and sit with you in your losses without judgment.

GROW groups are essential. They keep you grounded. They keep you honest. They keep you sane.

But they are not where you find clients.

They are not where you maintain authority.

They are not where you go to be seen as the expert.

And the moment you expect them to be all of those things, you'll end up frustrated, resentful, and wondering why the people closest to you don't take you seriously.

It's not their fault. You showed them everything. And everything is too much information for someone to also see you as the polished authority.

Once I understood that, the next realization came fast.

I needed new rooms. Rooms where no one had seen the messy middle. Rooms where I could walk in as the authority I'd become, not the woman who was still becoming.

I needed what I started calling SHOW groups.

A SHOW group is a group where you're intentional about how you show up. You keep an arm's distance. You share your expertise, not your uncertainty. You're generous with your knowledge but strategic with your vulnerability.

These are the rooms where your ideal clients are. The rooms where people meet you and think, "Wow, she really knows her stuff." The rooms where your authority is intact because proximity hasn't had time to erode it.

You're the shiny new object in a SHOW group. And let's be honest—it's fun to be the new kid. People are curious about you. They want to know your story. They see the highlight reel, the credentials, the results—not the two years of figuring it out that got you there.

That's not being fake. That's being strategic.

You're not lying about who you are. You're choosing what to lead with. And there's a massive difference between the two.

Think about it this way.

When you go to a doctor, you want to know they're qualified. You want to see the degrees on the wall. You want them to speak with confidence about your diagnosis.

You do not want them to say, "Well, I almost failed my anatomy class, and honestly my first year of residency was a disaster, but I eventually figured it out."

That might be true. It might even be endearing in a different context. But in that moment, in that room, it would destroy your confidence in them.

That's the difference between a GROW conversation and a SHOW conversation.

Your GROW group gets the anatomy story. Your SHOW group gets the degrees on the wall.

Both are real. Both are you. But they serve completely different purposes.

Now here's the part that tripped me up for years—and it might be tripping you up too.

Letting go of a GROW group feels like betrayal.

I was a member of one specific group for years. Years. I loved those women. I'd grown so much inside that community. They'd seen me through professional whiplash—joining as a paid speaker, then starting a networking company, then going back to speaking and coaching. They were on the whole ride with me.

But I kept having this fear that if I left, they'd essentially disown me. Like I was abandoning them. Like leaving meant I thought I was better than them.

Such a silly thought. But hey, I'm being honest.

When I finally had a hard conversation with myself, I realized two things. First, I had gotten too comfortable there. The group had become a habit, not a strategy. And second, I didn't even have the time to attend meetings anymore. I was holding on out of loyalty and fear—not because it was serving my business.

So I left.

And guess what?

The world didn't end.

Most members didn't even know I was gone. The ones I'd built real relationships with? They didn't go anywhere. I just wasn't paying to talk to them anymore.

It was a great group. It served its purpose beautifully. But sometimes you have to spread your wings and try new things. That doesn't mean the old things were bad. It means you grew—and growth sometimes means the room changes.

So how do you know which is which? How do you look at the communities you're in right now and figure out which ones are GROW groups and which ones need to be SHOW groups?

Here's what I ask myself now—and what I'd encourage you to ask too.

How long have I been in this room? If you've been in a community for years and the members have watched your entire evolution, that's a GROW group. They've seen too much for you to be the polished authority. That doesn't make the group less valuable—it just means you know what it's for.

Do the people in this room come to me for free advice but never hire me? That's a GROW group telling you it's a GROW group. The people who pick your brain over coffee and then hire someone they know less well? That's proximity at work. Stop expecting clients from that room and start appreciating it for what it actually gives you—support, perspective, and honest feedback.

When I walk into this room, do people see my expertise or my journey? If they see your expertise first—if they know you by your results, your reputation, your credentials—that's a SHOW group. If they see your journey first—if they know you by your struggles, your pivots, your "figuring it out" phase—that's a GROW group.

Could I be vulnerable in this room without it costing me credibility? If the answer is yes, it's a GROW group. If the answer is "probably not, and I wouldn't want to test it," that's a SHOW group. And that's fine. You don't need to be vulnerable in every room. You need to be vulnerable in the right rooms.

Am I the expert in this room, or am I one of many? SHOW groups work best when you bring something the room doesn't already have. If you're one of five speaking coaches in the group, you're competing for authority instead of holding it. Find rooms where your expertise stands out.

Here's the thing nobody tells you about this framework: you need both. Desperately.

If you only have SHOW groups, you'll burn out. You'll be performing all the time. You'll have no one to call when things fall apart, no one to be honest with, no one who knows the real you behind the authority. You'll feel isolated and exhausted, which is exactly what happens to a lot of women who "make it" and then feel completely alone at the top.

If you only have GROW groups, you'll stall out. You'll be surrounded by support but invisible to the people who need to hire you. You'll be the most loved, most respected, most helpful person in every room—and none of it will translate to revenue. You'll feel appreciated but undervalued. Seen but not sought out.

Sound familiar? It should. That was my entire Chapter 8 experience. I was helpful but not hirable because every room I was in was a GROW room. I had no SHOW rooms at all.

The balance between the two is what makes this work.

GROW groups keep you grounded, honest, and human. SHOW groups keep your authority intact, your pipeline full, and your business growing.

You don't have to choose. You have to be intentional.

And I want to be clear about something—because I know how this might sound.

This is not about being different people in different rooms. It's not about being fake or manipulative or putting on a mask.

It's about being appropriate.

You don't tell your therapist the same things you tell your boss. You don't talk to your best friend the same way you talk to a new client. You don't show up to a first date the same way you show up to a Tuesday night on the couch with your husband.

That's not being fake. That's being a human who understands context.

GROW and SHOW is just context—applied to your business.

And once you see it, you can't unsee it.

You'll walk into a networking event and know within ten minutes whether it's a GROW room or a SHOW room. You'll meet someone at a conference and instinctively know whether this is a person who gets the messy middle or a person who needs to see the authority.

That instinct? You already have it. You've just never had permission to use it.

Consider this your permission.

So now that you have the permission—what do you actually do with it?

Because understanding the difference between GROW and SHOW is one thing. Redesigning how you move through your business because of it is another.

Let me walk you through what it looks like when you realize you've been too close for too long—and how to strategically rebuild.

It usually starts with a feeling.

Clients have slowed down. Speaking gigs have dried up. You're showing up everywhere but opportunities aren't increasing. Everyone feels like they know you—and that's the problem.

You've become wallpaper. Familiar, comfortable, and completely invisible.

This is the moment most women push harder. They show up more. Post more. Network more. Say yes to more coffee chats. Join another group. Offer another free workshop.

Don't do that.

This is actually the moment to pull back.

I know that sounds counterintuitive. Everything you've been taught says the answer is more visibility. But you don't have a visibility problem. You have a proximity problem. And more visibility in the same rooms with the same people will only make it worse.

This is the moment you get strategic.

The first move is to sort your rooms.

Look at every community, group, networking organization, and online space you're currently in. Be honest with yourself. For each one, ask the questions we talked about earlier—how long have I been here, do they see my expertise or my journey, am I getting clients from this room or just coffee chats?

Then make your lists. Which rooms are GROW? Which rooms could be SHOW? And which rooms are you staying in out of loyalty, habit, or guilt—even though they're not serving either purpose anymore?

The rooms that are clearly GROW—keep them. Love them. Show up when you can. But stop expecting business from them. Stop giving your best content away for free in those rooms. Stop treating every conversation there like a potential client meeting. Let your GROW groups be what they are—support, friendship, honest feedback—and stop asking them to also be your sales pipeline.

The rooms that aren't serving either purpose? The ones you're staying in because leaving feels scary or because you've "always been a member"? Give yourself permission to leave. Remember what I learned—the world doesn't end. The people who matter will still be there. You're just not paying to talk to them anymore.

And now—this is the important part—go find new rooms.

New communities. New organizations. New spaces where nobody has seen your messy middle. Where you can walk in as the authority you've become and keep it that way.

These are your SHOW groups. And you need to treat them differently from the start.

Show up with intention. Lead with expertise, not vulnerability. Be generous with your knowledge but protective of your time. Build the kind of distance that signals value without creating walls.

You're the new kid. You're the shiny object. Use that strategically—because that window doesn't last forever.

The second move is to build an authority plan.

Not a visibility plan. An authority plan. There's a difference.

A visibility plan says: how do I get more people to see me?

An authority plan says: what can I create or accomplish that positions me as the expert—and then who needs to see it?

This is where you get intentional about the kind of visibility you're building. Authority-based visibility. The kind that compounds. The kind that works for you even when you're not in the room.

Apply for TEDx. Enroll in WHEN Stories. Write a book—a real one, not a lead magnet disguised as a book. Go on a podcast tour, but not just any podcasts—find the ones where your ideal clients are listening. Pitch credible publications and submit articles that showcase your expertise. Not a photo. Not a "featured in" badge. An actual article with your name on it that demonstrates why you're the authority in your space.

When it's published, share it everywhere. Not because you want the likes. Because you want the right people to see you doing the work that backs up the claim.

This kind of visibility takes longer. It's harder. It requires you to actually produce something—a talk, a book, an article, a body of work—instead of just posting a selfie with a ring light.

But it compounds. Every authority-based asset you create builds on the last one. The WHEN Stories leads to the podcast tour. The podcast tour leads to the book. The book leads to the stages. The stages lead to the clients who never would have found you in a networking group.

Each one moves you further from "seen" and closer to "known."

The third move is to protect your calendar like it's sacred.

Because it is.

When you were in full GROW mode—showing up everywhere, saying yes to everything, being the most available person in every room—your calendar was a free-for-all. Coffee chats. Brain-picking sessions. Quick calls that turned into hour-long coaching sessions. Your time was everyone else's resource.

Not anymore.

You're busy now. Not fake busy. Not "sorry, I'm booked" busy for the sake of appearances. Actually busy—building authority assets, serving paying clients, showing up strategically in your SHOW groups, and doing the work that positions you for the next level.

Your calendar doesn't have thirty open slots for anyone who wants to "pick your brain." It has space for paying clients, strategic relationships, and the GROW group people who keep you sane.

That's it.

This isn't about being a jerk. It's about being honest. Your time is your most valuable asset, and every hour you give away for free is an hour that reinforces the idea that your expertise isn't worth paying for. We covered this in Chapter 7. We covered this in Chapter 8. And now you have the framework to actually do something about it.

Set office hours if you want to stay accessible. Create a paid consultation for people who want your expertise. Direct brain-picking requests to your content—your podcast, your book, your published articles. Give them access to your knowledge without giving them access to your calendar.

Now—here's the hard part. The part where ego-centric visibility is going to tempt you.

Because ego-centric visibility is faster. It's easier. It gives you the dopamine hit of engagement and the illusion of progress almost immediately.

It's the paid magazine cover that looks impressive but teaches nobody anything about your expertise. It's the Times Square billboard that your friends will screenshot but your ideal clients will never see. It's the "bestseller" badge you bought but didn't earn.

And look—I'm not saying you can never do any of those things. There are moments where ego-centric visibility has its place. A nice headshot on a magazine is fine. A social media post celebrating a win is fine.

But if that's the *foundation* of your visibility strategy? If the majority of your visibility moves are about being *seen* rather than being *known for something*? People will see right through it. And instead of building trust, you'll start generating the one thing that kills authority faster than anything: skepticism.

She must be paying for all of that.

What does she actually do?

All sizzle, no steak.

That's what happens when ego-centric visibility outpaces your authority. People start to question you instead of trust you. And once trust erodes, no amount of visibility will get it back.

So yes, share the wins. Post the photos. Celebrate the milestones.

But make sure there's substance underneath it. Make sure that for every ego-centric visibility move, you've got three authority-based moves holding it up. The article. The talk. The book. The framework. The results. The body of work that makes people say "she's the real deal" instead of "she's really good at marketing."

This isn't an overnight transformation. I want to be honest about that.

You don't sort your rooms, build an authority plan, and lock down your calendar in a weekend. It's a process. It's uncomfortable. There will be moments where you feel guilty for pulling back. Moments where the old people-pleaser in you wants to say yes to the coffee chat. Moments where the ego-centric visibility opportunity lands in your inbox and it looks really, really shiny.

Stay the course.

Every boundary you hold is a message to yourself and to the market: my expertise has value. My time has value. My authority is real.

And over time—not overnight, but over time—the right people start to notice. The clients who are willing to pay. The event planners who seek you out. The podcast hosts who pitch you instead of the other way around.

Speakers, I'm going to hold your hand when I say this to you—event planners can spot ego-centric visibility a mile away, and they are rolling their eyes at it. They want YOU on video speaking. They want podcast episodes they can listen to so they can hear your frameworks, your personality. They want a book that shows your expertise and that you're serious.

When an event planner who's looking to pay a speaker sees ego-centric visibility, they see someone who is trying too hard to *look* important—instead of *being* important.

Harsh? Yes. True? 100%.

That's what authority-based visibility does. It flips the dynamic from you chasing opportunities to opportunities finding you.

And that's when you know the invisible line is working in your favor instead of against you.

We simply cannot do this on our own. I've tried. I built a business thinking I could figure it all out by myself, and all it got me was burnout, an eroded reputation, and a whole lot of coffee chats that went nowhere.

You need people who see everything—the doubt, the mess, the late-night panic. Those people will save your sanity.

And you need people who only see what matters—the expertise, the results, the authority you've built. Those people will save your business.

GROW groups and SHOW groups.

Get them both right, and the invisible line stops being something that happens to you.

It becomes something you navigate by design.

CHAPTER 12

Seen or Known

The words we choose reveal the claims we're willing to make—and the ones we're not.

A few weeks ago, I posted a simple question on Facebook.

"Would you rather be SEEN or KNOWN?"

That's it. No context. No explanation. Just a graphic with scattered red paper hearts and a question I'd been turning over in my mind while writing this book.

I was curious. I thought I knew what people would say.

I was wrong.

The majority chose "seen."

And not by a small margin.

"Seen!" "Seen." "SEEN!" One after another.

But here's what caught my attention—it wasn't the word they chose. It was how they explained it.

"Seen because once you have seen me then you want to get to know me!!"

"If understood = seen then SEEN!"

"'Seen' feels like present tense and 'known' feels like past tense."

One woman wrote that being seen and being known were the same thing to her.

And one response stopped me in my tracks: "This has my wheels turning. I love a good pondering!"

Mine too. Because the more I read, the more I realized something was happening in these responses that went way deeper than a simple preference.

These women weren't choosing "seen" over "known."

They were redefining "seen" to mean what "known" used to mean.

And that distinction—that subtle, almost invisible shift in language—unlocked something I'd been trying to understand for years about why the visibility conversation feels so broken.

Let me back up for a second.

Think about what "seen" used to mean. The basic, original, no-frills definition.

Seen is passive. It means someone looked at you. Their eyes landed on you. You appeared in their field of vision. That's it. You were *seen* the way a billboard is seen. The way a post is seen. The way a stranger on the street is seen.

There's no depth to it. No relationship. No understanding. Just visual contact.

Now think about what "known" means.

Known is active. It means someone understands you. They've spent time with your ideas, your work, your story. They associate your name with something specific. They could describe you to someone else without looking at your Instagram bio.

Known implies depth. Relationship. Trust. Reputation.

If I asked you right now—would you rather your ideal client *see* you or *know* you?—the answer should be obvious. You want them to know you. To understand what you do, why you're great at it, and why they should hire you instead of someone else.

So why did so many smart, capable women instinctively reach for "seen"?

Here's what I think happened. And this is where it gets philosophical, so bear with me.

The online business world broke the word "visible."

For years, every coach, every marketing guru, every business strategist told women the same thing: you need to be more visible. Get visible. Increase your visibility. Visibility is the key to everything.

Post more. Go live more. Show your face more. Be in more rooms. Get on more stages. Launch a podcast. Start a YouTube channel. Be everywhere.

Visibility became the holy grail of online business. And because everyone was saying it, the word got used so much that it stopped meaning anything. It became white noise. Just another piece of advice that felt both urgent and useless at the same time.

So women—smart, intuitive women who could feel that "visible" wasn't quite the right word for what they actually wanted—upgraded.

They reached for "seen."

Because "seen" felt different. It felt more personal. More human. More meaningful. It wasn't about algorithms and impressions and reach. It was about someone actually *looking* at you. Recognizing you. Understanding you.

"Visible" felt like marketing. "Seen" felt like connection.

And I get that. I feel that, too.

But here's what happened in the process: "seen" absorbed the meaning that used to belong to "known." And "known" got left behind—abandoned as a word that felt too cold, too strategic, too corporate for what women were actually trying to express.

The whole vocabulary shifted one word to the left.

"Visible" became meaningless noise.

"Seen" absorbed the emotional depth that "known" used to carry.

And "known"—the word that actually describes what every woman in business needs—got left on the shelf, gathering dust.

This might sound like I'm being overly analytical about word choice. Like I'm splitting hairs on a Facebook post. But I've spent this entire book showing you that words matter. That the difference between "writer" and "author" is the difference between hiding and claiming. That the difference between "I just help people" and "I'm an expert" is the difference between being overlooked and being hired.

The words we choose reveal the claims we're willing to make.

And when women collectively choose "seen" over "known," they're revealing something important about their relationship with authority and visibility.

They want depth. They want understanding. They want someone to look past the surface and see the real them.

But they're reaching for a word that doesn't require them to *build* anything. "Seen" is something that happens to you. Someone else does the seeing. You just have to show up and be looked at.

"Known" is something you earn. It requires you to create a body of work, develop expertise, build a reputation. It requires you to put something into the world that people can engage with deeply enough to form a real understanding of who you are and what you bring.

"Seen" is passive. "Known" is a claim.

And claims—as we've established over the last eleven chapters—are where we get squirmy.

There's another layer to this that I can't stop thinking about.

Several women in the comments described "seen" as something more intimate, more pure than "known." One woman said, "When someone fully sees you, they already know you. It seems more pure."

And I understand that feeling completely. In personal relationships, being "seen" does carry that depth. When your best friend sees you—really sees you—it means she understands you at a level that goes beyond facts and credentials. She sees your heart. Your intentions. Your fears.

That's beautiful. And it's real.

But in business, that level of being "seen" is exactly what erodes authority.

Think about it through the lens of everything we've covered in this book.

When your GROW group "sees" you—really sees you, all of you, the mess and the magic—they lose the ability to see you as the authority. That's not their fault. It's proximity. They've seen too much.

When your ideal client "sees" you in the way these women described—deeply, personally, fully—that's not a client relationship. That's a friendship. And as Chapter 8 taught us, the friend never gets the contract.

The kind of "seen" these women were describing is beautiful for personal relationships. But in business, it's the very thing that makes you helpful but not hirable.

What builds a business isn't being *seen* at a soul level.

What builds a business is being *known* for something specific.

I want to sit with this for a moment because I think it's one of the most important distinctions in this entire book.

There's a difference between being understood as a person and being recognized as an authority.

Both matter. Both are valuable. Both feed something real inside you.

But they serve different purposes. And when you conflate them—when you try to get both from the same audience, in the same rooms, using the same strategy—you end up with neither.

You end up being deeply "seen" by people who love you but don't hire you. And completely unknown to the people who would.

That's the gap. That's where so many women in business are living right now.

They are profoundly seen by their peers. Their GROW groups know them inside and out. Their networking communities adore them. Their social media followers feel connected to them.

And they can't figure out why none of it is translating to revenue.

It's because being seen and being known aren't the same thing. And the business world needs you to be known.

Not known the way your best friend knows you. Known the way your ideal client recognizes you—as the authority in your space. The person whose name comes up when your topic comes up. The person who doesn't need to explain her credentials because her reputation already did it for her.

That kind of known isn't cold. It isn't clinical. It isn't the opposite of being seen.

It's actually the deeper thing. It's what lasts after the scroll. After the event. After the coffee chat. It's what makes someone say your name in a room you're not even in.

One of the responses on my post said, "I want to be seen so I can be known. So if I have to pick just one, I'd pick seen."

She was describing a journey—seen first, then known—like seen is the doorway and known is the room. And on the surface, that makes total sense. People have to notice you before they can understand you. You have to appear in someone's world before they can engage with your work.

But here's where the invisible line shows up again.

If "being seen" is your primary strategy—if your focus is on getting more eyeballs, more impressions, more visibility—you can spend years being seen by thousands of people who never actually know what you do.

You become a familiar face with no clear value attached.

You become the woman everyone recognizes at the networking event but nobody refers.

You become helpful but not hirable.

That was my Chapter 8 story. I was seen everywhere. Known for nothing specific.

The path actually works better in reverse.

Be known first. Build the expertise. Create the authority-based assets—the book, the talk, the stage, the framework. Develop a reputation for something specific and valuable.

Then let the visibility follow.

Because when you're known for something, being seen amplifies it. Every post, every stage, every interview reinforces what people already believe about you—that you're the person to go to for this specific thing.

But when you're just seen—without being known for anything specific—more visibility just makes you more familiar. And as we covered in The Golden Ticket, familiarity without authority erodes your value.

Known creates pull. People seek you out.

Seen creates presence. People scroll past you.

You want both. But the order matters.

Authority first. Visibility second.

We've been saying it since Chapter 9. But now you have the language to understand why.

Here's what I think is really going on underneath all of this—and it's the thing I keep coming back to as I write this book.

Women don't reach for "seen" because they're confused about definitions. They're smart. They know the difference between being looked at and being understood.

They reach for "seen" because "known" feels dangerous.

To be known is to be exposed. To be known is to have people form opinions about you that you can't control. To be known is to step out from behind the safe, warm, passive experience of being "seen" and into the vulnerable, public, claimable experience of being recognized as someone who stands for something.

And we know what happens when women claim things. We've spent this whole book talking about it.

The invisible line appears.

People react.

The temperature changes.

So "seen" feels safer. Not because it's the right word. But because it doesn't trigger the line.

You can be "seen" without anyone feeling threatened by you. You can be "seen" and still be one of the group. You can be "seen" without risking the backlash that comes with being *known* as an authority.

"Seen" lets you stay on the safe side of the invisible line while still feeling like you're making progress.

But you're not. Not really. You're just being visible. And visibility without authority is a hamster wheel.

So here's what I want you to think about.

If someone in your industry heard your name tomorrow, what would they associate with it?

Not your face. Not your logo. Not the color of your brand.

What would they say you *do*? What would they say you're the go-to person for?

If you can answer that clearly—if there's a specific expertise, a specific contribution, a specific body of work that people connect to your name—you're known. And being known is the foundation that makes every visibility move you make actually count.

If you can't answer that clearly—if people know your face but not your thing, if they recognize you but couldn't explain what you do—you're seen. And no amount of additional visibility will fix that. More posts won't fix it. More networking won't fix it. More content, more reels, more coffee chats, more free workshops won't fix it.

You don't have a visibility problem.

You have an authority problem.

And the only way to solve it is to build something worth being known for—and then have the courage to claim it.

I know. There's that word again. Claim.

We've been circling it since Chapter 3. The flinch. The "just." The deflection. The refusal to call ourselves what we are.

And here it is showing up again, disguised as a preference for a softer word on a Facebook post.

I told you in Chapter 3 that the words we choose reveal the claims we're willing to make. "Writer" instead of "author." "I help people" instead of "I'm an expert." And now—"seen" instead of "known."

Every time, we reach for the word that doesn't require us to stand in our authority.

Every time, we choose the passive over the active. The soft over the bold. The safe over the claimed.

And every time, we wonder why we're not getting the results we want.

Here's what I'm not saying: I'm not saying those women on my Facebook post were wrong. I'm not saying "seen" is a bad word or a bad desire. I understand what they meant. I feel the pull of it too—the desire to be deeply understood, personally recognized, truly valued for who you are.

That's a beautiful, human thing to want.

But I am saying this: wanting to be seen is not a business strategy. And confusing the emotional desire to be understood with the professional need to be recognized as an authority is why so many brilliant women are exhausted, overexposed, and underpaid.

You deserve to be seen—deeply, personally, fully—by the people who love you. Your GROW group. Your Sara. Your inner circle.

And you deserve to be known—clearly, specifically, powerfully—by the people who need to hire you. Your SHOW group. Your ideal clients. Your industry.

Both are real. Both matter.

But they're not the same thing.

And the woman who knows the difference?

She stops chasing visibility and starts building authority.

She stops asking "how do I get more people to see me?" and starts asking "what do I want to be known for?"

And that shift—that one question—changes everything.

CHAPTER 13

Your Story Is Big Enough

Authority isn't built by hiding who you are. It's built by owning it.

"I don't think my story is big enough."

If I had a quarter for every time a woman said that to me, I'd be sitting somewhere tropical while writing this book instead of in my jammies, on my couch with my lab, Vinnie, panting a little too loudly for me to fully concentrate.

Here's an area of life where size doesn't matter.

I've had women on my stage who have had deeply traumatic stories—loss, abuse, tragedy. And I've had women who have lived pretty average lives with big ah-ha moments. They all matter. Every single one.

Yet they reduce themselves over and over.

"My story isn't big enough."

"My story is too heavy."

"Nobody wants to hear about that."

"I don't have one of those dramatic, movie-worthy moments."

Sound familiar? It should. It's the "just" pattern from Chapter 6 wearing a different outfit. I'm *just* a writer, not an author. My story *just* isn't that interesting. I *just* help people with their websites.

Same flinch. Same shrinking. Same refusal to claim what's right in front of them.

Now, I find it ironic in a way that I've spent several chapters talking about proximity and being cautious about telling all your dirty laundry to the SHOW group. About keeping an arm's distance. About strategic vulnerability.

So how do I now turn around and say "tell your story on stage"?

Here's the nuance. And this is important.

Creating a talk, a WHEN Story, that considers you're a whole-ass human with a whole-ass life behind you that led to this very moment in your career—it matters. People want to relate to you. They want to know there's a real person behind the expertise.

But the difference is this: you are walking them *through* the story. They aren't living it with you.

That's a massive distinction.

In your GROW group, people lived your story alongside you. They watched you figure it out in real time. They saw the mess as it was happening. That's why proximity eroded your authority there—they had too much access to the process.

On a stage, in a book, on a podcast—you're *curating* the story. You're choosing what to share, how to frame it, and where it leads. The audience gets to peek into what life was like for you and how you overcame or discovered something about yourself. They get the highlight reel of your humanity—not the unedited footage.

And that curated vulnerability? It doesn't erode authority. It builds it.

Because now you're not just the expert. You're the expert they understand. The expert they relate to. The expert they trust—not just because of your credentials, but because they've seen the human behind them.

Those stories always tell me something about who you are and why you do what you do now.

I like to say it's my magic trick. My superpower. You can tell me any random story about your life and tell me what your business is—and I can connect the dots.

Tell me a story about mice dropping out of the ceiling of a house you rented while in college, and I'll tell you what I heard: you're someone who makes decisive moves. You can handle a problem that literally falls in your lap. And your clients appreciate how you're good in the moment.

There's always a through-line.

We build confidence, courage, and resilience as we go. Life puts a moment in your path and you do the thing—that builds confidence. Then another moment comes and you do the thing again—that builds courage. And before you know it, you've got a trail of moments behind you that tell a story about exactly who you are and why you're qualified to do what you do.

You just haven't connected the dots yet.

That's what I do. I help you see the dots. And then I help you draw the line between them—from the moment everything changed to the authority you hold now.

One story stands out to me.

Kristin Adkins builds websites for speakers. Her business is Crash Design Co., and she is the authority on speaker websites, hands down. I send all of my speaking clients to Kristin when they need to create or update their websites.

Kristin was in the very first cohort of WHEN Stories speakers. As she was building her story, she was talking to the group and telling us a little more in depth about her relationship with her dad.

Kristin's dad passed away much younger than he should have.

She found herself sitting in the funeral home, in a very beige room, trying to put her dad's life story neatly on one page for his obituary.

One page.

A whole life—everything he was, everything he meant, everything he did—reduced to a few paragraphs in a beige room.

As she continued to tell us her story, I had this realization about why she does what she does.

She inherently wanted to tell her dad's full story but didn't have enough room. She couldn't possibly tell the world who he fully was in a few paragraphs.

Now, think about what Kristin does.

She literally builds websites for people so the world knows who they are.

Her WHEN Story—the moment everything changed—happened before she became the authority in speaker websites. But it was the seed. The thing that made her care so deeply about telling people's stories in a way that does them justice. A way that gives them more than one page in a beige room.

She didn't see that connection until we found it together.

Now imagine you're a speaker, and you stumble upon Kristin's WHEN Story. You hear about the moment everything changed for her, and then you learn about what she does—and why.

The dots connect.

You relate.

You understand her.

And you still see her as the authority. Even more so. Because now she's a human with a human experience AND she's the expert you need.

Her story didn't diminish her authority. It deepened it.

That's what a WHEN Story does. It doesn't replace your credentials. It gives your credentials a heartbeat.

This is the part of the visibility conversation that almost nobody gets right.

The online business world will tell you to "show up authentically." To "be vulnerable." To "share your story."

And then in the next breath, they'll tell you to post your wins, flex your revenue, and make sure everyone sees how successful you are.

It's contradictory advice. And it leaves women stuck in a terrible middle ground—oversharing their struggles in a way that erodes their authority, or performing their success in a way that feels hollow and attracts the wrong kind of attention.

The answer isn't one or the other.

The answer is a story that connects who you are to what you do—told with intention, from a place of ownership, not from a place of processing.

That last part matters. There's a difference between sharing a story you've made sense of and dumping a story you're still in the middle of. The first builds connection and authority. The second builds sympathy—and sympathy is not what gets you hired.

Your GROW group is where you process. Your SHOW group—and your stage, your book, your podcast—is where you share what you've already made sense of.

So what does it actually look like to own your story and claim your authority at the same time?

It starts with the moment. The WHEN. Not your whole life story. Not your résumé. Not a chronological walk through every job you've ever had.

One moment. The moment everything changed.

Maybe it's the moment you realized your career wasn't working anymore. Maybe it's the moment someone said something that rewired how you think. Maybe it's the moment you failed spectacularly and found something unexpected on the other side. Maybe it's mice falling from a ceiling.

It doesn't have to be dramatic. It doesn't have to be tragic. It doesn't have to be "big enough" by whatever arbitrary standard you've been measuring it against.

It has to be *yours*. And it has to connect to why you do what you do now.

That's the through-line. That's the thing that turns a random life moment into an authority-building asset.

When women take the WHEN Stories stage, you have to own the stage. Which means you have to own the story.

And I want to be honest with you—that's the hardest part.

Not the writing. Not the memorizing. Not the nerves of standing in front of an audience.

The hardest part is believing your story matters enough to tell.

Because we've been so conditioned to shrink—to say "just," to deflect, to minimize—that standing on a stage and saying "let me tell you about the moment everything changed for me" feels like the boldest act of authority some of these women have ever performed.

And it is.

That's the point.

The stage isn't just a visibility tool. It's a claiming tool. It's the moment you stop saying "I'm just a writer" and start saying "I'm an author." It's the moment you stop hiding behind your credentials and start standing beside them—with the full weight of your humanity backing you up.

During coaching, it's my job to make sure you see the whole story so you can own it. I want to help you step into your authority. Not just onstage. In your business. In your pricing. In the rooms you walk into. In the way you introduce yourself.

It was the moment Paquita Reddish—a woman who left an abusive marriage and chose herself and her children—took her last few words, stepped to the front of the stage, and claimed, "I am ready."

That moment changed her. It changed her business. And now she has also learned what it means to step over that invisible line.

Because here's what happens after women tell their WHEN Story:

They don't go back to shrinking.

Something shifts. Something clicks. They've stood on a stage and claimed their moment in front of a room full of people, and they survived. The world didn't end. Nobody called them arrogant. Nobody said they were "too much."

People cried. People connected. People said "I need to work with you."

And suddenly, the invisible line doesn't feel so scary anymore.

Because they're not just standing on the other side of it.

They're standing in their authority.

And they're not apologizing for it.

Your story is big enough.

I promise you, whatever moment is sitting in the back of your mind right now—the one you keep dismissing, the one you think nobody would care about, the one you've never told because it doesn't feel "impressive" enough—that's the one.

That's your WHEN.

And it's been waiting for you to claim it.

CHAPTER 14

The Temperature Changed

The invisible line doesn't go away. You get faster at seeing it.

Not long ago, I noticed something that made my stomach tighten.

Similar-looking stages started to pop up. Storytelling stages. In theaters. With nice lighting. Built around personal stories.

My first reaction wasn't pretty.

Here we go again.

It brought me right back to the Kindness Bucket Brigade. The look-alike Facebook groups. The people who started their own versions and proudly positioned themselves as doing it "the right way" or the less expensive way. That old, familiar feeling of someone taking something I built and running with it.

I felt the heat rise. The annoyance. The urge to screenshot and send it to someone with a "can you believe this?" caption.

And then I stopped.

I've written this book. I've done the research. I've sat with the psychology. I've turned the mirror on myself and told you to do the same. So I had to ask myself the same question I asked you in Chapter 10:

What is this bringing up in me right now?

Here's what I realized—and it didn't take long, which is the whole point.

What I built with WHEN Stories came from a deep place inside me. It took over a year to curate. I live it, breathe it, work it every single day. It's my framework. My ecosystem. My coaching. My stage.

And it's okay for someone else to take something that might look similar and do their own thing with it.

Because when it comes down to it—it's not the same at all. Because it's not me. It's not my story, my process, my years of building the invisible line framework that lives underneath every part of WHEN Stories. It's a similar stage. Nothing more, nothing less.

And it's okay.

This is where I realized I was being the asshole.

I was judging what someone else was doing because it felt like we were in first grade and I'd drawn a picture of a house, a tree, a yellow flower, and a family of four—only to look over and see the little girl next to me also drew a yellow flower.

And suddenly that yellow flower felt like a personal attack.

At fifty years old, I was having a first-grade reaction to someone else's yellow flower.

I'm telling you this because I want you to know something: I don't have this figured out.

I'm not writing this book from the mountaintop. I'm writing it from the middle.

I'm fifty years old, and I'm just like everyone else—learning to see things differently, judge less, understand myself a little deeper, and question myself more than others.

I'm also trying to unlearn all the bullshit I've consumed over the years around authority, visibility, and proximity. The messages that told me to be everywhere, be available, be humble, don't brag, don't charge too much, don't get too big for your britches.

That unlearning doesn't happen overnight. It happens in moments—small, uncomfortable moments where you catch yourself reacting and choose to respond instead.

The copycat stage was one of those moments.

And the fact that I caught it—that I didn't stay in the annoyance, didn't spiral, didn't make it mean something it didn't—is progress.

Not perfection. Progress.

So let's talk about what you actually do when the temperature changes. Because it will. Everything in this book has been building to this truth: the invisible line doesn't go away when you're able to see it.

People will still react when you grow.

Friends will still pull away.

Whispers will still find their way back to you.

Someone will still look at what you've built and decide you're "too much" or "too big" or "too full of yourself."

And you will still feel it. In your gut. In the room. In the silence that's just a little too long.

The difference now is that you have the language for what's happening. And language changes everything.

The first thing to do when you feel the temperature change is the hardest: don't react. Sit with it.

I know. Every instinct in your body will want to do something. Fix it. Confront it. Shrink yourself back to where things were comfortable. Call someone and vent. Post something passive-aggressive. Or—the most common one—immediately start questioning what you did wrong.

Don't do any of that. Not yet.

Give yourself twenty-four hours to just feel it. Name it. Use the language you now have.

Is this the invisible line? Did I just cross it—and is someone reacting to the shift?

Is this proximity? Have I been too close to these people for too long, and my growth is disrupting the equilibrium?

Is this the moralization of discomfort? Is someone turning their feelings about my success into a moral judgment about my character?

Or—and this is the one that takes the most courage—is this me? Am I the one having a reaction to someone else's growth? Am I drawing the invisible line around them because their success is bringing something up in me?

Name it. That's the first step. Because once you name it, it stops controlling you.

The second thing to do is check which group you're in.

This sounds simple, but it's where most of the damage happens.

If the temperature changed in your GROW group—in the community where people have seen everything, where you've been vulnerable, where the proximity is close—take a breath. This is expected. You've outgrown the room, or you're growing faster than the room, and the dynamics are shifting because of it. That doesn't mean the relationships are over. It means the relationships are changing. And change is uncomfortable for everyone, not just you.

You don't have to burn it down. You don't have to leave dramatically. You might just need to adjust your expectations. Stop looking for clients in that room. Stop expecting to be seen as the authority there. Let it be what it is—a GROW group—and find your authority elsewhere.

If the temperature changed in your SHOW group—in a space where you've been strategic, where you've maintained distance, where people primarily know you through your expertise—pay closer attention. Something shifted. Maybe you shared too much. Maybe you got too comfortable and the line between GROW and SHOW blurred. Or maybe you just crossed the invisible line by getting a win that disrupted someone's perception of the hierarchy.

Either way, the fix isn't to shrink. The fix is to get clearer about how you're showing up and whether you're maintaining the distance that protects your authority in that space.

The third thing is the one nobody wants to hear: let people go.

Not everyone is going to make the journey with you. Some people loved you at one level and won't know how to love you at the next. Some friendships were built on you being peers, and when you cross the line into authority, the foundation cracks.

That doesn't make them bad people. It doesn't make you a bad person. It makes you someone who grew.

And growth has a cost. I wish I could tell you it doesn't. I wish I could say you get to keep everyone. But the truth is, some people will fall away. Some will go quietly. Some will go loudly. And some will go in ways that break your heart.

Let them.

Not with anger. Not with resentment. With understanding. You know what's happening now. You have the language for it. They probably don't. They're feeling something they can't name, and they're doing the best they can with the discomfort—even if their best looks like gossip, distance, or silence.

You can hold compassion for them and still keep growing.

Those two things aren't in conflict.

The fourth thing—and this is the one I want you to carry with you long after you put this book down—is to keep going.

Not in a "hustle harder" way. Not in a "prove them wrong" way.

In a "this is who I am and what I've built and I'm not apologizing for it" way.

Every chapter of this book has been about a different version of the same moment: the moment a woman crosses the invisible line and has to decide what to do on the other side.

Shrink or grow.

Apologize or own it.

Retreat or stand.

And every time I've told you one of my stories—the Kindness Bucket Brigade, the networking years, the WHEN Stories stage, the copycat stages—I've shown you both choices. Because I've made both. I've shrunk, and I've stood. I've retreated, and I've claimed.

The difference now isn't that I always choose correctly.

The difference is that I choose faster.

I catch the flinch before it becomes a retreat. I name the dynamic before it becomes a spiral. I feel the temperature change, and I don't immediately assume I did something wrong.

That's what this book has given you. Not perfection. Not immunity. Not some magical shield that protects you from the invisible line.

It's given you speed. The ability to see it, name it, and choose—in real time—how you want to respond.

I had a moment recently where I was coaching a speaker and she said something that stopped me cold.

She said, "I just don't want people to think I've changed."

And I looked at her and said, "But you have changed. That's the whole point. You've grown. You've built something. You know things now that you didn't know before. Why would you want people to think you're the same?"

She got quiet.

Then she said, "Because if I've changed, they might not like me anymore."

And there it was. The invisible line. Not drawn by other people. Drawn by her. On herself. To keep herself small enough to be liked.

I told her what I'm going to tell you:

The people who only like the version of you that stays small were never your people.

Your people—your *real* people—will celebrate your growth even when it makes them uncomfortable. They'll adjust. They'll rise with you. They'll figure out how to stay in relationship with the new version of you because the relationship matters more than the hierarchy.

And the ones who can't do that?

You already know what to do.

Let them go. Wish them well. And keep going.

Because you didn't come this far to draw the invisible line on yourself.

CHAPTER 15

I'm the Founder

The invisible line doesn't stop showing up. You just stop letting it stop you.

There's something I've been avoiding.

Not in this book—I think we've been pretty honest with each other by now. But in my life. In my business. In the way I introduce myself.

I've been avoiding the word "founder." Sure, I've typed it, but I really haven't embraced it fully.

This is ridiculous when you think about it. I've spent an entire book talking about why women avoid claiming authority. I walked you through the flinch with "author." I showed you the "just" pattern. I made you turn the mirror on yourself.

And here I am, at the end of this book, still squirming at a word.

Founder.

It feels too big. Too official. Too much like I'm saying "I built something that matters"—which, apparently, is still hard for me to say out loud even after writing fifteen chapters about why it shouldn't be.

But I did build something that matters. And it's time I said it.

I used to be Wendy Babcock, International and TEDx Speaker, Author, and Speaker Coach.

That was my identity for years. And I was proud of it. Every word in that title was earned—the stages, the TEDx, the books, the clients. I built that title one uncomfortable step at a time.

But something shifted when WHEN Stories came to life.

WHEN Stories became my WHEN moment.

It changed everything.

It went from a daydream at my desk to a full business with cohorts, stages, anthologies, podcasts, a YouTube channel, and a team. It went from "I wonder if this could work" to four events in under a year. It went from an idea my marketing coach didn't get to a movement she celebrated.

And somewhere in the middle of all that building, I crossed the invisible line again.

Because I wasn't just coaching speakers anymore. I wasn't just helping people tell their stories. I was building something bigger than me—something that could exist and grow and impact people even when I wasn't in the room.

That's a founder.

And I've been dodging that word the same way I dodged "author" back in 2019.

I knew I was the bottleneck of my business. As long as WHEN Stories only existed when I was personally coaching every speaker, personally running every event, personally touching every story—it could only grow as fast as I could work.

So I changed it.

I created Certified WHEN Stories™ Facilitators—women who could host my stage in their cities, run their own cohorts, walk speakers through the frameworks I'd built. My goal was to have two facilitators by the end of 2026.

I enrolled three facilitators before the end of 2025.

Now they're hosting their own cohorts. Helping women step into their stories. Creating authority-building assets in communities I've never even been to.

My frameworks. My stage. My vision. Their cities. Their speakers. Their impact.

That's not coaching. That's not speaking. That's not even just a business.

That's a legacy.

And *legacy* is a word that makes me even more uncomfortable than *founder*.

I struggle with claiming this. I want you to know that. I'm not standing at the end of this book pretending I've conquered the flinch.

I still catch myself wanting to say "I just run a little coaching business" when someone asks what I do. I still deflect when speakers thank me on stage. I still have moments where I think, *Who am I to call myself a founder?*

But I'm getting faster at catching it.

That's what this whole book has been about. Not perfection. Speed. The ability to feel the flinch and choose differently before it pulls you back across the line.

I couldn't have gotten here without Sara.

Sara Deacon is my Publishing House Director and Chief Editor. She's my right hand. My business bestie and my bestie bestie.

She keeps me in check.

Those moments I shared throughout this book—the ones I wasn't proud of, the reactions I'm still learning from—sometimes Sara wants to go to bat for me. She'll read a comment or hear about something someone said, and her first instinct is to fight. And I love her for that.

But other times, she quietly reminds me to take a breath and reflect on why I might be feeling a certain way. She doesn't dismiss it. She doesn't tell me I'm wrong. She just holds up the mirror—gently—and lets me see what I need to see.

Everyone needs a Sara.

I used to surround myself with people I fully showed up for who didn't give much back to me in return. I used to people-please to death. I used to pour everything into relationships that drained me and call it generosity.

Sara is the friend and business bestie I wish everyone had. She listens. She talks through ideas without putting them down, even when I'm on a tangent rambling about some big new thing I want to build. She tells me the truth when I need to hear it. And she reminds me—over and over—that I'm the authority. That I should hold my boundaries. That it's okay to say no.

She's my GROW person. The one who sees everything and still believes in what I'm building.

And because I have her, I can walk into my SHOW rooms and be the *founder*. I'm not doing it alone.

We simply cannot do this on our own. I've said it before and I'll say it again.

Having people around you that support you, but also call you out on your own bullshit—that's a blessing.

It certainly doesn't hurt to have a husband so supportive that he took on a woodworking side hustle building the WHEN letters for the stage. He hauls the chair, the rug, and the letters he made for each event. He makes sure I drink water during events and keeps me sane.

When I look back at the woman who started this journey—the little girl in Mr. Kennedy's classroom, the nervous speaker giving a 60-second introduction she didn't know how to finish, the woman who started a kindness group and watched it nearly destroy her—I barely recognize her.

Not because she's gone. She's not. She's still in here. Every flinch, every "just," every deflected compliment—that's her. Still trying to stay small enough to be safe.

But she's not running the show anymore.

The woman running the show is the one who built a stage from a daydream. Who created frameworks that other women now use to change lives. Who enrolled three certified facilitators when she only hoped for two. Who sat on her couch in her pajamas with a panting lab named Vinnie and wrote an entire book about the thing nobody else was talking about.

The invisible line.

The line between being cheered on and being scrutinized. Between peer and authority. Between "You go, girl" and "Who the hell does she think she is?"

I've crossed it more times than I can count. And every single time, it cost me something. Friendships. Peace of mind. Confidence. Sleep.

But it also gave me something.

It gave me this book. This business. This stage. This life.

And it gave me the understanding that the line isn't the enemy. The line is the evidence. Evidence that you're growing. Evidence that you're building something. Evidence that you've stepped into authority that matters.

The only real danger is letting the line stop you.

So here's where I leave you.

You're going to put this book down and walk back into your life. Into your business, your communities, your networking groups, your social media feeds.

And at some point—maybe tomorrow, maybe next week, maybe in the middle of a launch or a pitch or a conversation with someone you thought was safe—you're going to feel it.

The temperature will change.

Someone will say something. Or stop saying something. The energy will shift. The room will feel different. And that old familiar feeling will rise up in your chest—the one that says, *What did I do wrong?*

When that happens, I want you to remember this book.

Not every chapter. Not every framework. Not every story.

Just this:

You didn't do anything wrong. You grew. And growth makes people uncomfortable—including, sometimes, yourself.

The invisible line is real. It will always be there. And the people on the other side of it will always have something to say about the fact that you crossed it.

Cross it anyway.

You've now been officially warned about visibility, authority, and the bullshit no one talks about... until now.

Own the word. Claim the title. Take the stage. Build the thing. Charge what you're worth. Stop saying "just." Stop handing your credit to someone else. Stop drawing the invisible line on yourself.

You *are* the authority.

Now go be the founder of whatever it is you're building.

I'm Wendy Babcock.

I'm the founder of WHEN Stories™.

What's Next

If this book moved something in you—if you saw yourself in these pages, if you finally have language for what you've been feeling—here's where to find me.

WHEN Stories™

The TEDx-style stage for personal stories. Six weeks of story development coaching, a live stage experience, a published anthology, a stand-alone Legacy book, podcast feature, and professionally produced video. If you're ready to stop saying "just" and start claiming your authority, this is where it happens.

Certified WHEN Stories™ Facilitator Program

Want to bring WHEN Stories to your city? This program trains women to host WHEN Stories stages, run cohorts, and build authority-building experiences in their own communities. If you're a coach, speaker, or facilitator who wants to create something bigger than yourself, let's talk.

The Legendary Women in Business Conference

My annual live event where women entrepreneurs come together to learn, connect, and stop apologizing for their success. Visit legendarywib.com

Connect With Me

Website: wendybabcock.com or whenstories.com

If you loved this book, the single best thing you can do is tell another woman about it. Send her the link. Tag me in your post. Leave a review. Not for my ego—for her. Because somewhere out there, a woman is sitting in a networking group wondering why being helpful isn't working. She needs this book. Help her find it.

A Note on Sources

This book is built on personal experience—but the patterns I describe are backed by real research. Here are the key concepts and their origins for readers who want to go deeper.

Tall Poppy Syndrome (Chapters 5, 14): A well-documented social phenomenon describing the tendency to criticize, resent, or undermine people who achieve visible success. The term originates from a Roman legend attributed to Tarquinius Superbus and has been studied extensively in Australian, Canadian, and workplace psychology contexts. For a comprehensive overview, see the work of Dr. Rumeet Billan and the Tall Poppy Syndrome research conducted through the Thomson Reuters Foundation.

Social Identity Theory (Chapter 5): Developed by social psychologists Henri Tajfel and John Turner in the 1970s and 1980s. The theory explains how people categorize themselves and others into in-groups and out-groups, and how these categorizations shape perception, behavior, and judgment. Key works include Tajfel's *Human Groups and Social Categories* (1981) and Turner's *Rediscovering the Social Group* (1987).

The Double Bind (Chapter 2): Research on competing expectations placed on women in leadership, particularly the conflict between being perceived as competent and being perceived as likable. Foundational work in this area includes Alice Eagly and Linda Carli's *Through the Labyrinth: The Truth About How Women Become Leaders* (2007) and Catalyst's extensive research reports on the double bind in professional settings.

Moralization of Discomfort (Chapters 5, 10): The psychological tendency to reframe emotional discomfort as moral judgment—turning "I feel uncomfortable" into "you did something wrong." This concept draws from moral psychology research, particularly the work of Jonathan Haidt on moral emotions and post-hoc moral reasoning in *The Righteous Mind* (2012).

Social Correction (Chapter 5): The phenomenon of peer groups using criticism, doubt, or subtle undermining to bring a rising member back to the perceived group level. This connects to broader research on social norms enforcement and status threat in group dynamics.

Authority and the Latin Root *Auctor* (Chapter 3): The etymological connection between "author" and "authority" traces back to the Latin *auctor*, meaning originator or creator. This linguistic connection is well established in etymological references and has been explored in various works on the philosophy of authorship and intellectual ownership.

These sources informed my thinking, but this book is not an academic text. It's a field guide—written from the middle of the experience, not from a distance. If any of these concepts resonate with you, I encourage you to explore the original research. The more language you have for what's happening, the faster you can navigate it.

Acknowledgments

This book almost didn't happen. Not because I didn't have the material—I've been living it for decades. But because writing a book about claiming authority requires you to actually claim it. And as you now know, that's the part I'm still working on.

So let me start with the person who wouldn't let me quit.

Sara Deacon—my Publishing House Director, Chief Editor, business bestie, and the best friend I've ever had. WHEN Stories™ exists because you helped me build it. I don't know what I did to deserve you, but I'm not giving you back.

To Brian—my husband, my biggest fan, and the man who built the WHEN letters for the stage with his own hands. You hauled the chair. You hauled the rug. You made sure I drank water at every event. You never once questioned why I needed to write this book at midnight in my pajamas with Vinnie and Dexter panting (or roo'ing) next to me. You just made me coffee and let me work. I love you more than I can put into words, which is saying something considering I just wrote 32,000 of them.

To my daughters—you've watched me build, fail, rebuild, and keep going. I hope this book shows you that it's okay to be "too much." Be too much. The world needs it. So go stake your claim on who you are in this world.

To Will Bowen—you gave me my first stage, my first training, and my first real understanding of what it means to show up with a message. Your program changed the trajectory of my life. *The Complaint Free World* movement led me to every stage, every story, and eventually to WHEN Stories™. Thank you for seeing something in that email from a medical coder in Wisconsin.

To Alexis Caldicott—you asked me the one question that changed everything: "What do people come to you for advice about?" That question built a business. Thank you for making me pause when I wanted to jump. It's the reason WHEN Stories became the empire I'm building.

To Kristin Adkins, Paquita Reddish, and every woman who has stood on the WHEN Stories stage—you trusted me with your moments. You let me help you find the through-line. And then you stood under those lights and claimed it. You are the reason this work matters. Every single one of you made me a better coach, a better storyteller, and a braver founder.

To my Certified WHEN Stories Facilitators: Lisa Condon, Michelle Vande Hey, Sharon Slack and those yet to come on board—you took what I built and carried it into rooms I've never even been in. You believed in the vision and said yes before you knew if it would work or not. You're helping me build a legacy. And I'm still getting used to saying that out loud.

To the women in the networking groups, the masterminds, the Facebook communities, the coffee chats—even the ones who pulled away—you taught me what the invisible line looks like from every angle. Some of those lessons hurt. All of them mattered.

And to Vinnie—my lab, my couch companion, my loudest breather—and Dexter—my Samoyed, the ultimate roo'er and fluffy puppy—You were here for every single chapter. You didn't understand a word of it, but your presence made the writing less lonely. Good boys.

About the author

Wendy Babcock is the founder of WHEN Stories™—a multi-platform storytelling and visibility experience where women entrepreneurs step onto a live theatre stage, share their defining moment, and transform it into authority assets including books, podcast features, and professionally produced video.

An award-winning songwriter who found her voice after years of trauma, Wendy understands the psychological shift that happens when you stop trying to be liked... and start becoming known. Her work centers on authority-based visibility—the difference between chasing attention and building credibility that compounds.

Through WHEN Stories™, Wendy has helped women cross what she calls *The Invisible Line*—the moment when you are no longer seen as a peer, but as a leader. Her approach blends storytelling, business strategy, and identity transformation to help women become not just visible, but undeniable.

She is a Forbes Entrepreneur of Impact nominee and recipient of the Small Business of the Year Award, and her work has been featured across podcasts, live events, and national media.

Wendy lives in Wisconsin and believes legacy is built when your story becomes an asset—not a secret.

To learn more, visit wendybabcock.com and whenstories.com.